FOOTBALL
THE GAME AND RULES

BY STANLEY LOVER

Foreword by
Michel Zen-Ruffinen
GENERAL SECRETARY, FIFA

Illustrations by Joe Colquhoun and Stanley Lover

Including
THE LAWS OF THE GAME
and
DECISIONS
of the
INTERNATIONAL FOOTBALL ASSOCIATION BOARD

CHAMELEON

Author's note

Football – The Game and Rules is a completely revised and updated version of its predecessor *Soccer Laws Illustrated*. Published in many languages around the world it has been an established text book for over a quarter of a century.

Football – The Game and Rules is updated with new material to explain the way in which football is intended to be played to preserve the beauty of the game around the world. It answers many questions on the meanings and interpretations of the rules in play through more than 100 clear action illustrations and diagrams.

Football – The Game and Rules does this with the minimum of text and includes guidelines for players, coaches, Referees, organizers and supporters.

Much care has been taken to base the contents of this work on the official text of the Laws of the Game and Decisions of the International Football Board which are included in full. The author is indebted to FIFA for encouragement and co-operation in according permission to reproduce the Laws of the Game and other FIFA-related material.

Also by Stanley Lover:	*Soccer Rules Explained*	*Soccer Laws Illustrated*
	Soccer Match Control	*Soccer Judge*
	Soccer and Its Rules	*Illustrated Soccer Quiz Book*
	Fair Play Guide	*You are the Ref!*

First published in 1971 by Pelham Books
This edition first published in Great Britain in 1999
by Chameleon Books an imprint of André Deutsch Ltd
76 Dean Street
London W1V 5HA
www.vci.co.uk

A catalogue record for this book is available from the British Library

ISBN 0 233 99658 3

Printed and bound by MPG Books Ltd, Bodmin, Cornwall

10 9 8 7 6 5 4 3 2 1

Design by Design 23

Cover photographs © Empics   .

CONTENTS
KICK-OFF TO FINAL WHISTLE

For the Good of the Game

FOOTBALL – THE PEOPLE'S GAME

In praise of Football. Football has been described as *The People's Game* because it appeals to millions of people bound together in a world football family. It is a joy to play because each player can express personal skills in an exciting sport. It is a joy to watch because the ball is always visible and the play easy to follow.

Football is at its best when a game flows from goal to goal and when the players display their skills in a spirit of fair play, respecting opponents, officials and faithful supporters while creating a thrilling experience.

To make the most of each football game requires a basic knowledge of the rules. Players need to know what is fair and unfair to avoid offences which stop the play, give the ball to the opponents, and frustrate their own skills. Coaches and club officials need to know enough to be able to set correct disciplines on and off the field. For parents and friends of football a basic knowledge will help to understand and enjoy *The People's Game* better.

The purpose of this book is to provide a visual link between the legalistic text of the official rules and the excitement of actual play. The complete formal Laws of the Game are included for readers who wish to know more.

FOREWORD

The rules of any sport should be clear and easy to apply. In football we are fortunate to have just seventeen, founded on basic concepts which have stood the test of time in life and in play. Our set of simple rules has established football as the world's most popular sport giving pleasure to all members of the family. Even so, where individual passions are touched, we are drawn into discussion, controversy and disagreement, about how these rules are, or should be, applied.

It is FIFA's endless quest to achieve consistency of interpretation and application of the formal Laws of the Game. Perfection will remain elusive, as in so many things in life, for the play is guided on the field by human beings – Referees – with all of the individualistic quirks that this implies. Whatever differences of opinion may arise FIFA holds fast to the sporting ethic that the decisions of a neutral arbiter, on facts connected with the play, are *final*.

To reduce areas of controversy FIFA welcomes publications, such as this one by an acknowledged expert on the game and its rules. It is a visual link between the written rules and the play. It is a guide, not only to the application of the rules, but also to the roles of all members of the football family on how to safeguard the true values of fair play in our sport.

Fair Play is Better Play.

Michel Zen-Ruffinen
General Secretary of FIFA

FIFA

For the Good of the Game

PREFACE

Ken Aston, International Referee; Past Chairman, FIFA Referees' Committee and Member of the International Football Association Board

Over 200 countries, more than in the United Nations, are members of FIFA, which administrates the game of football. In truth, football is the World Game. It attracts players of all ages because it is a simple and enjoyable activity. It requires minimum and inexpensive equipment and all the things which the physically fit like to do are implicit in the game.

Running, jumping, bodily contact and, above all, kicking an object are all part of a sporting 'war game' where the object is to capture (and recapture) the enemy's stronghold — his goal.

Just as there are rules of war, to limit excesses and which should be honoured (but sometimes aren't), so there are rules of the game which should be observed (but sometimes aren't) to ensure the safety of the players and provide the maximum of enjoyment for them and spectators alike.

Football has been played in its present form since 1863 but the rules have changed very little in their basic principles. Most of the changes in detail, particularly in recent years, have tended to recognize the increasing pace of play and advances in technology. Although players and spectators have a general grasp of the rules there is no doubt that a better understanding of their purpose and application will add to the pleasures of the game. Conversely, a poor or mistaken interpretation often provokes unjust criticism of referees' decisions with consequent loss of enjoyment. Referees make fewer errors than is generally supposed. They study hard to apply the spirit of the rules, as well as the letter, to enable games to be played in a sporting climate.

This book will help towards a better appreciation of the game, its rules, and the part all football people can play to keep it a clean and healthy sport.

Ken Aston MBE

THE SPIRIT OF THE GAME

Football is more than a simple game. It is an emotional experience. The mechanics of the play amount to the movement of a ball, about the size of a man's head, between two targets set some distance apart. But, in the course of just one game, the whole range of human emotions, from the depths of despair to utter joy, can be touched in the hearts of those who play or watch.

Somewhere in these emotions lies the key to the 'spirit of the game', a term often mentioned but rarely defined. To merely present in these pages a series of illustrations of the written rules without considering the spirit in which they are intended to be applied would offer an unfinished story.

The spirit in which the game should be played was considered more important than the written rule by the nineteenth-century founders of the game of Association Football. A few rules, or Laws as they were styled, were set down to regulate the physical play but there was not a word on the principles or ethics to be observed. In those days it was not necessary to write down a code of conduct. After all, the game as we know it today was devised by men steeped in the codes of ethics and gentlemanly conduct imposed by the strict era of Queen Victoria.

Much wisdom was included in those few early rules because the game has remained practically unchanged for over 130 years. Both early and subsequent legislators have carefully guarded the inner soul of football when considering alterations. A close look at the reasoning behind the written rules provides three important clues to the interpretation of the 'spirit of the game' in the form of the basic principles:

Equal opportunity. All players must have an equal opportunity to demonstrate individual skills without unfair interference from opponents. Physical size or brute strength is not an essential element for success. Players of small stature can show their skills, by quick reactions and balance, alongside others whose assets include height and strength. Many players of small physique have achieved world fame by showing their exciting skills.

Safety. Playing the game involves physical contact which can be tough. The rules provide for the protection of players in certain specified situations, for protective equipment and treatment of injuries, and limit physical challenges for the ball.

Enjoyment. The rules are clear on what is unfair play and acts of misconduct which destroy skill and the pleasure of playing or watching the game. The purpose of the written rules is to provide a *stimulating and healthy* sport in which people of all ages can experience the maximum enjoyment.

Summarizing then, the basic principles of the 'spirit of the game' are simply: **Equality, safety, enjoyment.**

The governing body for the Laws of the Game, The International Football Association Board (IFAB), receives many suggestions intended to improve the game and to change the laws. The following statement, issued by the IFAB after the annual meeting in 1968, remains valid in today's game:

> 'It is the belief of the Board that the Spirit in which the Game is played is of paramount importance and that changes in the Law, to improve the Game as a spectacle, are of little value if 'fair play' is not universally observed.'

FAIR PLAY IN SPORT

Definition
Fair Play in sport is a code of conduct which respects both the written and unwritten rules of play. Opponents are accepted as partners in sport.
Fair Play is expressed through spontaneous actions which applaud sporting excellence, which show concern for opponents in distress, which acknowledge defeat with dignity and victory with humility.
Sport with fair play enriches the quality of life.

STANLEY F. LOVER

KICK-OFF – THE GAME OF FOOTBALL

The Game
Football (official title – Association Football) is a team game played by people of all ages. It is played for pure enjoyment in friendly games or competitively in matches between teams in organized tournaments.

Components
Essential components are: players, a ball, and space.

Object
The object of the game is to combine the skills of the players in a team effort to move the ball through the opponents' goal to score a goal.

Match Result
The team scoring the highest number of goals wins the match. If both teams score an equal number of goals, or if no goals are scored, the match is drawn.

Method of Play
To achieve a score each team attacks the opponents' goal, generally by a series of passing movements of the ball, using any part of the body (except hands or arms) to put the ball through the goal. Each team has a goalkeeper who is allowed to use hands to protect the goal.

Rules of Play
Matches are regulated by the Laws of the Game as decided by the International Football Association Board. These may be modified within approved limits for tournament play. Players are required to understand and respect the official Laws of the Game and any special tournament rules.

The Referee
To ensure that matches are played in accordance with the Laws and tournament rules a Referee is appointed to supervise the play inside the field. Assistant Referees, when available, supervise certain aspects of play from outside of the field boundary lines.

Decisions of the Referee
The decisions of the Referee regarding facts connected with play are final.

DEFINITION OF TERMS USED IN THE LAWS OF THE GAME

Advantage: At an offence the Referee may allow play to continue if it is to the advantage of the non-offending team.

Caution: A formal warning against further unfair play or unsporting behaviour. Indicated by a yellow card shown by the Referee.

Coach: A team official who may convey tactical instructions to the players during a match.

Dangerous play: Any action, considered by the Referee to be dangerous to another player, which is not a listed offence.

Free kick: 'The privilege of Kicking the Ball, without obstruction, in such a manner as the Kicker may think fit.' (This is the original definition of 1863. It remains valid in the modern game).

Goalkeeper: An identified player, in each team, permitted to touch the ball with the hands, inside the Penalty Area, to defend the goal.

Handling: Deliberate use of the hand or arm to influence the movement of the ball in play by a player other than the goalkeeper.

Impeding: An offence when a player, who is not playing the ball, impedes the progress of an opponent by interposing his body between the opponent and the ball.

Misconduct: Any act of misbehaviour contrary to the letter and spirit of the Laws of the Game.

Offside Position: A player is in an Offside Position if he is nearer to his opponents' goal line than the ball, unless (a) he is in his own half, or (b) level with the second last opponent, or (c) is level with the last two opponents. It is not an offence to be in an Offside Position.

Offside: An offence when a player is in an Offside Position and is judged, by the referee, to be interfering with the play, with an opponent, or gaining an advantage.

Scoring: A team scores a goal when the ball passes through the opposing team's goal in compliance with the Laws.

Tackling: A challenge made with the foot, either from the front or the side, to play the ball while in the possession of an opponent.

PART 1

COMPONENTS

Just four essential elements to start any match

COMPONENTS

A game of football does not need elaborate equipment. In kick-about games it is not even necessary to have a football! Many children make do with objects varying from bundles of rags tied with string, cartons and cans, to paper cups, shoes and caps! The playing area is any available space, be it in the streets, on a beach, in the playground or inside the home. What imagination! What fun! No need for rules in these games!

The formal *Laws of the Game* are for football players who want to play in friendly team games or in organized matches in competitions.

Much care has been devoted to setting down the basic components common to all matches, no matter where they may be played. Standard equipment is intended to minimize elements of danger and yet encourage maximum effort.

The first four laws detail the essentials – the playing field, the ball, the players and their equipment.

Football is played on a rectangular field to encourage the flow of play between the main targets, i.e. the goals.

The size of the field may be varied between given limits according to the space available. However, the named areas within the boundaries are of fixed dimensions.

The field is divided into two halves. Goal nets are advisable but not compulsory.

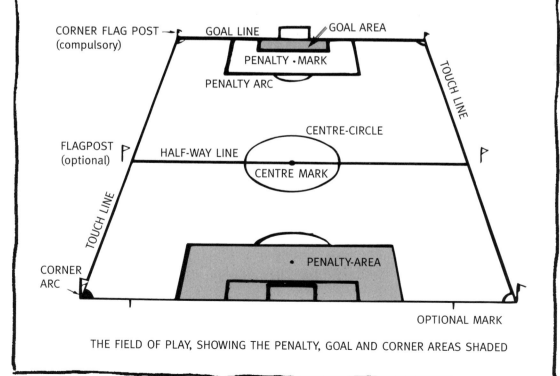

THE FIELD OF PLAY, SHOWING THE PENALTY, GOAL AND CORNER AREAS SHADED

15

THE GOAL

The size of the goal is related to the physical capability of the goalkeeper to defend the goal and to demand skill from attacking players to score.

The goalposts are white in colour so they can easily be seen. Goalnets are optional.

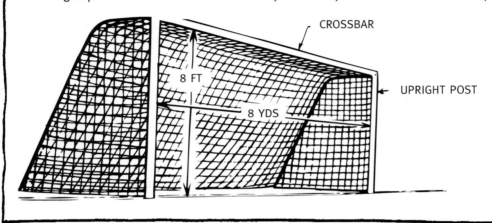

CROSSBAR

8 FT

8 YDS

UPRIGHT POST

**LINE MARKINGS
CORNER-ARC**

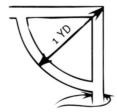

1 YD

CORNER FLAGPOST
(compulsory)

5 FT
MIN

2¹/2 – 3 INS LINE
WIDTH ADVISED
(up to 5 ins allowed)

(For metric
measurements see Law 1
on page 102)

HALFWAY FLAGPOST
(optional)

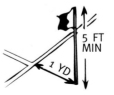

5 FT
MIN

1 YD

If, during a game, a crossbar is broken may it be replaced by a rope?

The use of a rope to replace the crossbar is not permitted. (Decision 1)

Flagpoles shorter than 5 feet (1.50m) are dangerous.

A spherical ball is chosen for the game of football because it truly reflects the skill of the player in kicking, heading, controlling or moving it in any manner permitted by the rules.

Its size, weight, pressure, and materials used in manufacture, are required to meet rigid FIFA standards.

 THE BALL

May the ball be changed during a game?
The ball may not be changed during the match without the authority of the Referee.

Advice
It is advisable to choose a match ball inflated to suit the conditions of play. Generally, a soft ball is preferred on a hard surface and a harder ball on a soft, or very wet surface.

Are all matches played with the same size of ball?
No. A smaller ball is advisable for young players.

In every match there are two teams each having not more than eleven players on the field.

Where competition rules permit, up to three substitutes may be used. In non-competiton games up to five substitutes may be used.

One player of each team is a goalkeeper with the privilege of handling the ball within his team's penalty area.

A team starts a match with only ten players. The eleventh player arrives at the commencement of the second half. May he join his team?

Yes, provided that the Referee is advised. If the game is in progress the player must wait for a signal from the Referee.

'A match may not start if either team consists of fewer than seven players' (Law 3).

A goalkeper is injured and wishes to change places with another player. Is this permitted?

Yes, at any time, provided that the Referee is advised when the change is to be made and that play has been stopped.

May a player, who has had to leave the field for treatment of an injury, return to his team?

Yes, after receiving a signal from the Referee.

What is the procedure for a substitute to join the game?

- There is a normal stoppage of play;
- the Referee is notified;
- the outgoing player has left the field;
- the Referee signals the new player to enter the field;
- the new player enters at the halfway line.

If a player is dismissed from the game for misconduct, may his place be taken by a substitute (No.12)?

A player who has been dismissed **after** a match has started can not be replaced. A player who has been sent off **before** the kick-off may be replaced only by one of the named substitutes.

The main points of this law are **safety** for the players and **correct presentation** on the field of play.

The basic compulsory equipment includes shinguards to protect the player's legs. In addition it is the player's responsibility not to wear anything which could be dangerous to himself or to any other player. To assist players in obtaining a secure foothold, footwear incorporating bars or studs is permitted but these must be checked regularly to minimize the element of danger to other players.

Goalkeepers must be clearly identified by wearing colours which avoid possible confusion with the other players, the Referee and Assistant Referees.

- Shirt

- Shorts

- Stockings

- Shinguards

- Footwear

Can any action be taken if a player advises the referee that an injury has been caused by the studs on an opponent's boot?

The Referee has power to examine players' footwear at any time and to instruct any player to leave the match to correct items considered to be dangerous.

The Referee may require a player to remove a ring or any other article which could cause injury.

May a player wear spectacles during a match?

The Laws do not prohibit spectacles. The obvious danger to the wearer, and to other players, should be clearly understood before the match commences.

A player decides to play without any footwear. Is this permitted?

No. Compulsory equipment includes footwear.

When a player has had to leave the field to correct some item of equipment, how may he rejoin the game?

The player must wait for a stoppage in the game before reporting to the Referee who will then examine the player's equipment and satisfy himself that everything is in order.

What would happen if a player, who has left the field with the Referee's permission to correct dangerous equipment, rejoins the game without waiting for play to be stopped?

The Referee is required to caution the player (Law 12, caution offence No. 6.) An indirect free kick is awarded to the opposing team.

Part 2

RULES OF PLAY

Basic procedures: getting started; duration of play; stops and restarts; scoring goals

RULES OF PLAY

Now that we have the essential components the game can begin. Like any other sport the rules of play for football deal with the method of playing the game – how to start and restart, timing, how to score, etc. Nine of the official laws deal with these rules of play.

The normal period of play is ninety minutes made up of two equal halves of forty-five minutes. These periods may be slightly reduced for young players. Where competition rules allow, extra time may be played in the event of there being no result at the end of the normal period.

When the game is delayed to allow an injured player to be examined, or removed from the field, the Referee will make allowances to compensate for the amount of time lost.

The Referee is required to make allowances for time lost during substitutions, dealing with offending players, or any other reason at the Referee's discretion.

As the Referee is about to signal the end of play a defender handles the ball in his own penalty area. What action must the Referee take?

A penalty kick must be awarded.

The Referee has authority to extend playing time to allow a penalty kick to be taken at the end of a normal period.

Note: If a defender denies an opponent an obvious goal opportunity (as here) the Referee is required, by Law 12, to dismiss the offending player.

If, at the end of the first period of play, the visiting team's captain asks the Referee to commence the second period without an interval, so that his team can start their return journey as early as possible, would this be in order?

The law entitles players to an interval, at half-time, not to exceed fifteen minutes. There is no minimum. If all players agree to a brief interval the Referee would be in order to consent unless a competition rule insists on a minimum period.

Each team defends one half of the field. The toss of a coin decides which team chooses the goal it wishes to attack, the other team will have first possession of the ball at the kick-off.

After the half-time interval the teams change ends. The second period of the match is started by a kick-off, taken by the team which did not start play in the first period. Play is also restarted with a kick-off after a goal has been scored.

To restart play after a temporary halt, for any cause not mentioned elsewhere in the Laws, the referee will drop the ball at the appropriate place.

Where should players stand at the kick-off?

Every player is in his own half of the field. Players of the team opposing the kick-off remain not less than ten yards from the ball until it is kicked and moves forward.

At a kick-off the ball is kicked directly into the opponents' goal. Is this a goal?

Yes. A goal may be scored directly from a kick-off. (Introduced in 1997.)

May a player kick the ball before it touches the ground when it is being dropped by the Referee?

No. The ball is not in play until it touches the ground. In this case the Referee would drop the ball again.

The boundary lines, i.e. goal lines and touch lines,
contain the game within a reasonable area to encourage
the flow of play between the goal targets.

The ball is out of play, and the game brought to a halt,
when the whole of the ball has crossed over a boundary
line, either on the ground or in the air.

The lines belong to the areas of which they are the
boundaries.

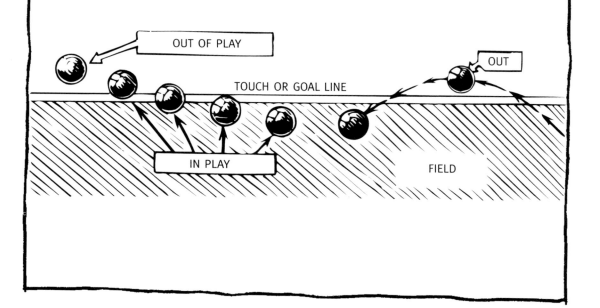

OUT OF PLAY

OUT

TOUCH OR GOAL LINE

IN PLAY

FIELD

Should play be stopped if the ball strikes the Referee?

No. Law 9 states that the ball is in play if 'it rebounds from either the Referee or an Assistant Referee when they are on the field of play'.

In the case shown here a goal would be awarded.

If the ball goes over the goal line, but is caught by the goalkeeper who is standing in the field of play, must the game be stopped?

Yes, if the ball has passed completely over the goal line. The position of the goalkeeper does not alter this fact.

'The team scoring the greater number of goals during a match is the winner. If both teams score an equal number of goals, or if no goals are scored, the match is drawn.'

To score a goal, the whole of the ball must pass over the goal line, between the posts and under the crossbar.

If the ball wholly crosses the goal line but returns into the field of play the goal is valid.

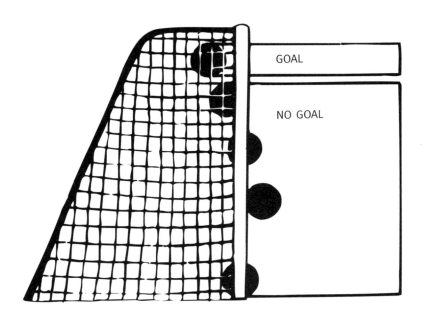

GOAL

NO GOAL

If the ball is about to enter the goal but is deflected by a dog (or spectator) can the Referee award a goal?

The revised laws, of 1997, do not refer to this eventuality but the traditional interpretation (in accordance with the spirit of the law) is not to allow a goal and to restart play by dropping the ball.

Would a goal be scored if a goalkeeper, standing in his own penalty area, throws the ball with the aid of a strong wind, into his opponents' goal without any other player touching the ball?

Yes. This is the only way in which an attacking player can score by the use of the hands.

Free kicks are awarded by the Referee to penalize infringements of the Laws. 'Free' means 'free from interference by players of the offending team'. They must not approach nearer to the ball than the limits imposed in the Laws until the ball has been kicked into play.

There are two types of free kick:

DIRECT: from which a goal can be scored against the opposing team when the ball passes directly into the goal.

INDIRECT: from which a goal can only be scored if the ball is touched or played by a player of either team, after it is kicked into play and before it enters the goal.

POSITION OF PLAYERS AT A FREE KICK

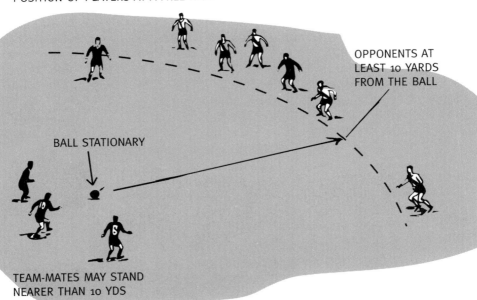

OPPONENTS AT LEAST 10 YARDS FROM THE BALL

BALL STATIONARY

TEAM-MATES MAY STAND NEARER THAN 10 YDS

If a defending player takes a direct free kick from outside his penalty area, and kicks the ball past his own goalkeeper into the goal, what would be the correct decision?

The Referee would award a corner kick to the attacking team, because a goal can only be scored against the **offending** team from a direct free kick.

How do players and spectators know if the free kick is direct or indirect?

When the Referee awards an indirect free kick he signals it by raising his arm. This signal precedes the blowing of the whistle for a free kick to be taken; no such signal is given in the case of a direct free kick.

From an indirect free kick if the ball goes directly into the opponents' goal a goal kick is awarded to the defending team.

May the defending players stand less than ten yards from the ball at any time?

Only when an indirect free kick is to be taken from a position less than ten yards from the goal. Defenders may stand on the goal line between the posts.

Is it in order for defending players to move nearer than ten yards when the signal is given?

Not until the ball has been kicked into play.

Note: At a free kick the kicker must not touch the ball a second time before it has touched another player.

If the defending team is awarded a free kick outside of their own penalty area may the ball be kicked to the goalkeeper?

Yes, but if the goalkeeper touches the ball with his hands, inside the penalty area, an indirect free kick (Law 12) is awarded to the opposing team.

From an indirect free kick the ball strikes the crossbar, hits the goalkeeper and bounces over the goal line. Would this be a goal?

Yes, because the ball was last played by a player other than the kicker before it entered the goal.

A penalty kick is an important award to punish any of ten offences, listed in Law 12, when committed by a player within his own team's penalty area.

Law 14 describes the requirements for the taking of a penalty kick. These include restrictions on the conduct of the kicker, the goalkeeper and the other players.

Playing time may be extended to allow a penalty kick to be taken (Law 7). The Referee decides when the penalty kick has been completed.

The players other than the kicker are located:
- inside the field of play
- outside the penalty area
- behind the penalty mark
- at least ten yards (9.15m) from the penalty mark
  The goalkeeper stands on the goal line between the posts.

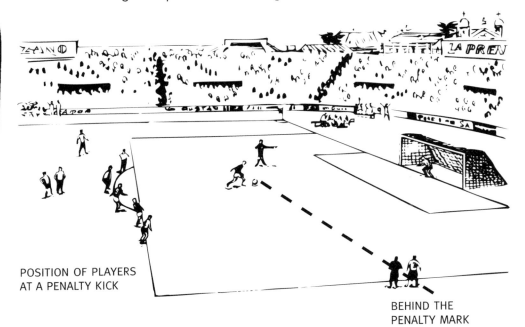

POSITION OF PLAYERS
AT A PENALTY KICK

BEHIND THE
PENALTY MARK

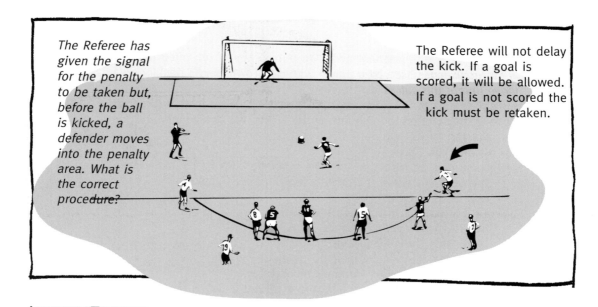

The Referee has given the signal for the penalty to be taken but, before the ball is kicked, a defender moves into the penalty area. What is the correct procedure?

The Referee will not delay the kick. If a goal is scored, it will be allowed. If a goal is not scored the kick must be retaken.

What would happen if a player of each team encroaches into the penalty area or within ten yards of the penalty mark before the ball is in play?

The penalty kick must be retaken.

Is the goalkeeper allowed to move before the ball is kicked?

Yes, along the goal line but not towards the ball.

Would a goal be allowed if the ball strikes the crossbar or goalpost and returns to the kicker who then kicks it into goal?

A goal would not be allowed because the kicker must not play the ball a second time until it has been touched by another player. The Referee would award an indirect free kick against the kicker.

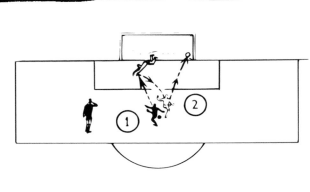

The Referee has extended time to allow a penalty kick to be taken. If the ball rebounds from the goalkeeper to the kicker, who scores, will the goal be allowed?

No. The game ends the moment the goalkeeper prevents the ball from entering the goal.

When the ball passes over a touch line the game is restarted by a throw-in awarded to the team opposite to that of the player who last touched the ball.

A goal can not be scored direct from a throw-in.

CORRECT THROW-IN.

FACING FIELD OF PLAY.
BOTH FEET ON GROUND,
ON OR BEHIND LINE.

INCORRECT.

ONE FOOT ON GROUND.

INCORRECT.

ONE HAND THROWING

CORRECT.

BOTH HANDS THROWING BALL.

Is this throw-in correct?

Yes, provided that the ball is thrown from behind and over the head, and that the action of throwing is continuous from the start of the throw to the point of release.

A defender takes a throw-in and throws the ball back to his goalkeeper. The ball goes directly into the goal before the goalkeeper touches it. Is it a goal?

No. A goal cannot be scored directly from a throw-in. In this case a corner kick is awarded to the opposing team.

When one of the attacking team plays the ball over the goal line, excluding the portion between the goalposts, the defending team is awarded a goal kick.

The ball is not in play until it has been kicked direct out of the penalty area. A goal may be scored direct from a goal kick.

CORRECT GOAL KICK

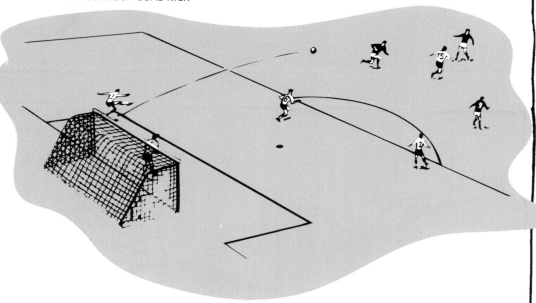

The ball is kicked from any point within the goal area when all opponents are outside of the penalty area.

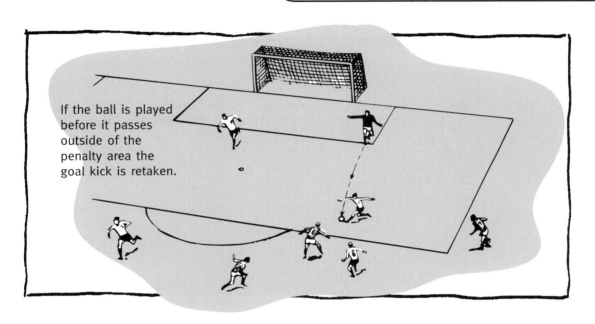

If the ball is played before it passes outside of the penalty area the goal kick is retaken.

If the ball is kicked over the goal line before it has cleared the penalty area, should the referee award a corner kick?

As the ball was not in play when it crossed the goal line, the goal kick must be retaken.

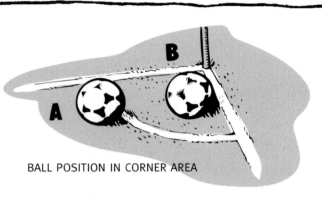

BALL POSITION IN CORNER AREA

When one of the defending team plays the ball over the goal line, excluding the portion between the goalposts, the attacking team is awarded a corner kick.

'The ball is placed inside the corner arc at the nearest corner flagpost.' B is clearly inside the arc. A is acceptable because it overlaps the corner arc line.

Would it be in order for the kicker to move the corner flag post?

The corner area provides ample room for a player to take a corner kick. The flagpost must not be moved.

Which positions may attackers and defenders take in relation to the ball at a corner kick?

Attackers may be as near to the ball as they wish, but defenders must be at least ten yards away.

If the ball is kicked against a goalpost and returns to the kicker, may he then play it again?

The kicker may not play the ball a second time until it has been touched by another player. An indirect free kick is awarded from where the ball was played for the second time by the kicker.

If the ball goes directly into goal from a corner kick would a goal be allowed?

Yes.

If the ball swerves over the goal line but back into play, should the game continue?

The moment the whole of the ball has crossed the goal line it is out of play. The game would be stopped and a goal kick awarded to the defending team.

Part 3

OFFSIDE

Simply explained and illustrated

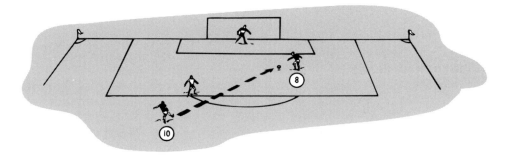

WHY OFFSIDE?

Football is a team game. The objective is to combine the skills of the players to move the ball through the opposing team's goal.
The principle of offside is important to this objective because it discourages any player from trying to gain an unfair advantage by being in advance of the ball, near to goal, to score with the minimum of effort.

Other team games, e.g. rugby, hockey, water polo, have an offside rule based on the same principle - that a player caught in front of the ball is considered out of play, off-the-side, offside. The player must not try to interfere with or influence the play in any way.

The Offside Rule demands alertness and intelligence from all players who must assess tactical movements and devise counter measures. It contributes much to the attractive fluidity of a football game.

This law is designed to discourage uninteresting play by attacking players. The game could be played without Law 11 but that might lead to players standing close to goal waiting for the ball for short-range attempts at scoring. Such play would require little skill or ability.

It is not a difficult law to understand if two basic points are clearly established. They are:

(a) a matter of FACT based on the actual position of the player *at the moment the ball is played* by one of his own side and,

(b) a matter of OPINION judged by his influence on the play and his motive for being in that position.

FACT: A player is in an OFFSIDE POSITION when he 'is nearer to his opponents' goal line than both the ball and the second last opponent'.

EXAMPLES:

OFFSIDE

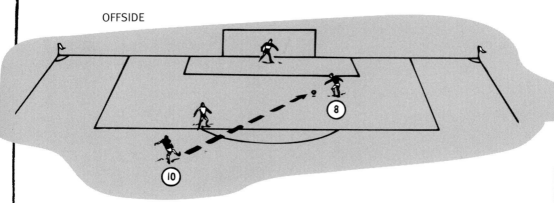

When No. 10 passes the ball forward No. 8 is in an OFFSIDE POSITION (having only one opponent between himself and the goal line). He is clearly involved in Active Play and is adjudged OFFSIDE.

The ball is thrown in and immediately played back to the thrower, who is now offside, being in front of the ball and having only one opponent between himself and the goal line.

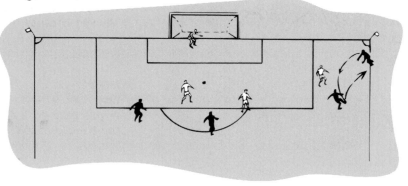

When No. 7 passes the ball No. 9 is at position A. He moves back to receive the ball at position B. He is adjudged offside because he was in an OFFSIDE POSITION when the ball was played by No. 7 (FACT) and is clearly gaining an advantage by being in that position (OPINION).

Note: When the ball is played by a team-mate a player can not put himself Onside by moving back from an OFFSIDE POSITION.

No. 6 kicks the ball towards the goal but it is deflected by an opponent to No. 9 who scores. The goal is not allowed because No. 9 was in an OFFSIDE POSITION, and involved in Active Play, at the moment the ball was kicked by No. 6. The deflection by the opponent in this case does not affect the basic principles of offside.

No. 8 shoots for goal. The ball rebounds from the crossbar to No. 11 who puts it into the goal. The goal is not valid because, although No. 11 was behind the ball when it hit the crossbar, he was in an OFFSIDE POSITION (having only one opponent nearer to the goal line) and gained an advantage from that position.

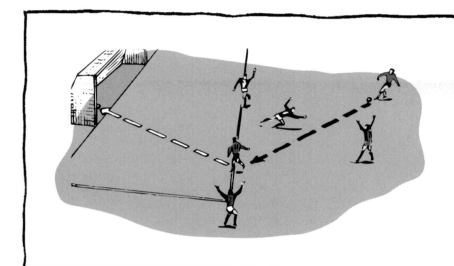

At the moment the ball is played towards No. 11 he is not in an offside position because he is level, or in line, with the two last opponents.

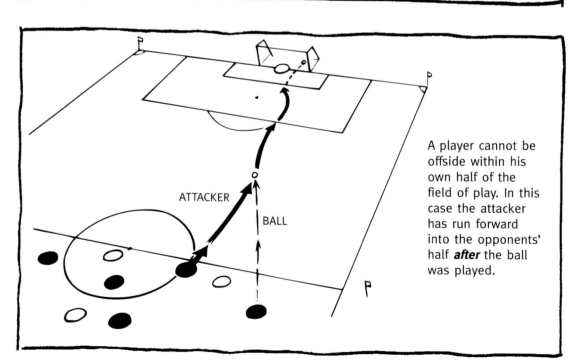

ATTACKER

BALL

A player cannot be offside within his own half of the field of play. In this case the attacker has run forward into the opponents' half *after* the ball was played.

No. 9 is not offside because he was not in front of the ball when it was last played by a team-mate.

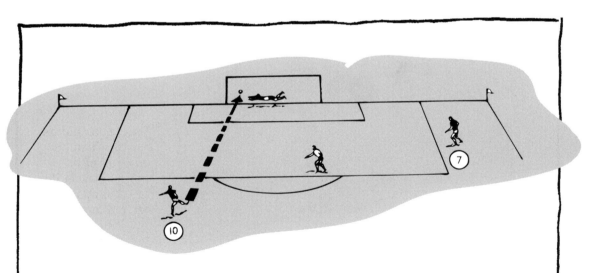

No. 7 is in an OFFSIDE POSITION when No. 10 kicks the ball into the goal. The goal is valid because No. 7 was not involved in Active Play.

No. 7 has moved to the ball from a forward pass. He was not in front of the ball when kicked by his team-mate and is therefore not offside.

A player can not be offside if he receives the ball direct from a corner kick, a goal kick or a throw-in.

A player can not be offside if he receives the ball direct from a throw-in. The goal is allowed.

Summarizing the offside law, in every possible situation only two questions need answering:

(i) Is the player in an OFFSIDE POSITION when the ball is played by one of his own side? (This is a matter of FACT.)

If the answer is 'Yes' then,
(ii) Is he interfering with play or an opponent, or gaining an advantage? (This is a matter of OPINION.)

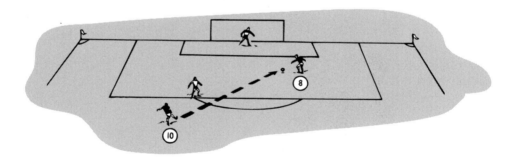

Part 4

FOULS AND MISCONDUCT

What not to do!
Offences and punishments

FOULS AND MISCONDUCT

At first sight Law 12 – *Fouls and Misconduct* – makes gloomy reading because it is concerned solely with punishing players. However, on reflection, it is at the heart of the game.

The three basic principles of the *'spirit of the game'* are clearly exposed in this law:

Equal opportunity, for all players to demonstrate their skills, is provided by severely restricting the degree of physical challenges for possession of the ball. To play fairly requires players to avoid challenges which are *careless, reckless, or involve excessive force.*

Safety, is evident in protecting players from dangerous play.

Enjoyment, in defining actions which are unacceptable in providing a healthy, fair, and exciting sport.

Law 12 comprises three parts:
  (i)   Major offences –   Diect free kick award
  (ii) Other offences – Indirect free kick award
  (iii) Misconduct offences – Caution or Dismissal

(I) MAJOR OFFENCES

Ten offences which are penalized by the award of a Direct free kick to the opposing team. Nine relate to physical acts against opponents, the tenth being illegally handling the ball.

A penalty kick is awarded if a player commits any of these offences inside his own penalty area.

EXAMPLES OF MAJOR OFFENCES –
DIRECT FREE KICK AWARD

KICKING AN OPPONENT

TRIPPING – USING THE LEGS

TRIPPING – BY STOOPING IN FRONT OF (OR BEHIND) AN OPPONENT

JUMPING AT AN OPPONENT
(the offending player clearly has no intention of playing the ball)

CHARGING IN A VIOLENT OR DANGEROUS MANNER

A CHARGE IN THE BACK CAN CAUSE SERIOUS INJURY

ATTEMPTING TO STRIKE AN OPPONENT IS PUNISHED AS IF CONTACT IS MADE

A GOALKEEPER WHO INTENTIONALLY THROWS THE BALL AT AN OPPONENT IS GUILTY OF STRIKING

PULLING AN OPPONENT'S SHIRT
IS A HOLDING OFFENCE

HOLDING WITH THE
HAND OR ARM

PUSHING AN OPPONENT

DELIBERATE HANDLING OF THE BALL: Deliberate handling of the ball with any part of a hand or arm. Exception: Does not apply to the goalkeeper handling the ball within his own penalty area.

FOUL TACKLE FROM BEHIND: A foul tackle, from behind, contact made with opponent before touching the ball. May be a cautionable or dismissal offence depending on the severity of contact.

KICKING AN OPPONENT: This illustrates a 'foot over' tackle, often interpreted as 'serious foul play' and requires dismissal of the offending player.

FAIR CHARGE

When trying to obtain possession of the ball it is fair to attempt to put an opponent off balance without using excessive force. Here is an example of a fair charge, shoulder to shoulder, arms and elbows close to the body, ball within playing distance.

UNINTENTIONAL HANDLING

An example of unintentional handling where the ball is kicked on to the hand. This is not an offence.

(II) OTHER OFFENCES

There are eight offences which are penalized by the award of an indirect free-kick to the opposing team. Five of these are directed to the goalkeeper with the main intention to release the ball into play with the minimum of delay.

The first three offences are:
(a) playing in a dangerous manner
(b) impeding the progress of an opponent
(c) preventing the goalkeeper from releasing the ball from his hands

(A) PLAYING IN A DANGEROUS MANNER

Attempting to kick a ball near the head of an opponent is dangerous.

An overhead 'bicycle' kick or a scissor kick, shown here, may be interpreted as dangerous play if attempted near other players.

(B) IMPEDING THE PROGRESS OF AN OPPONENT.

Opponents are entitled to make a fair challenge for possession of the ball. When not playing the ball it is an offence to impede (obstruct/ block) an opponent, by running between the opponent and the ball or interposing the body to block a challenge.

Even though the charge may be fair the ball is not within playing distance and the opponent is impeded from getting to it.

Impeding, or obstructing, by running between an opponent and the ball.

An example of 'screening' the ball from an opponent which is not 'impeding' because the ball is being played.

Obstruction is penalized when a player blocks the opponent's path to the ball when it is not within playing distance.

(C) PREVENTING THE GOALKEEPER FROM RELEASING THE BALL.

The goalkeeper is encouraged to release the ball from his hands, and into play, as soon as possible. It is an offence to prevent this by blocking his path.

GOALKEEPERS – RESTRICTIONS ON POSSESSION OF THE BALL

The role of the goalkeeper is to prevent the ball from passing through the goal. For this purpose the goalkeeper has the special privilege of touching the ball with the hands inside the penalty area. To discourage abuses, and with the object of making the ball available to the other players with the minimum of delay, Law 12 lists five offences specifically addressed to goalkeepers. They relate to excessive possession of the ball and restrictions on using the hands.

Use of the hands is not permitted from a direct pass, or from a throw-in, from a teammate. To avoid the risk of being penalized for wasting time goalkeepers are advised to release the ball within five to six seconds.

POSSESSION BY GOALKEEPER

The goalkeeper is allowed no more than four steps when controlling the ball with the hands before releasing it. After releasing the ball the goalkeeper is not allowed to touch it again with his hands until it has been played by another player. He may, however, play the ball with his feet.

A goalkeeper falls on the ball and makes no attempt to release it until an opponent has retreated. Is this in order?

No. The ball must be released within a reasonable time, usually five or six seconds.

Goalkeepers are not permited to touch the ball with the hands from a throw-in taken by a team-mate. An indirect free kick is awarded where the offence occurred.

(III) MISCONDUCT

Any player who disregards the principles of the Laws of the Game, by acts of discourtesy towards officials, persistently committing offences, or whose conduct offends the accepted code of fair play in sport, receives an official caution from the Referee. This is a warning not to repeat unsporting behaviour.

For offences of serious foul play, violent conduct, offensive, insulting or abusive language, repeated misconduct after receiving a caution, players are dismissed from a match. Other offences, in this category, include spitting at an opponent or any other person and denying an obvious goal-scoring opportunity to an opponent.

Misconduct of any kind, requiring the above sanctions, is reported to the appropriate authority (competition, regional, or national association, etc). Further disciplinary procedures may follow involving periods of suspension from playing and, in some cases, payment of fines.

The following examples illustrate some acts of misconduct which damage not only the individual reputations of the players concerned but also offend the true ideals of fair play.

Showing dissent, by word or action, from any decision given by the Referee. (Caution for first offence.)

Distracting, or attempting to distract, an opponent by shouting. Caution for unsporting behaviour. Indirect free kick to the opposing team.

Kicking the ball away from the place where the Referee indicates a free kick is to be taken, showing dissent from the decision or to delay the restart of play. (Caution.)

Foul play during a stoppage in the game. (Dismissal.)

An attacking player moves towards the goal with a clear chance to score but is tripped by a defender. In addition to awarding a penalty kick (the offence occurs inside the penalty area) the Referee dismisses the defender for denying an opponent an obvious goal-scoring opportunity. (Law 12: Sending-off offences No. 5.)

Misconduct to the Referee, at any time, even though it ocurs off the field of play, is dealt with as if it occurred during the game.

Misconduct towards an Assistant Referee (or Fourth Official) at any time before, during or after a match. (Caution or dismissal according to the offence.)

Part 5

PLAY TO THE WHISTLE

What the match officials have to do

PLAY TO THE WHISTLE

Match officials are not necessary in games played purely for fun and where the players control their own code of conduct, agree what is fair and unfair, just for the pleasure of kicking a ball among friends.

For organized matches, either as friendly games or in competitions, where the teams agree to play to the Laws of the Game, it is necessary to have a neutral person to decide points of contention and guide the conduct of the match within the rules.

Fully qualified Referees and Assistant Referees are trained experts in the interpretation and application of the laws.

The Referee is delegated many duties and responsibilities by match organizers. Effectively, the Referee is a superintendent appointed to manage, direct and control a football match. Any issue which directly touches on the conduct of a match must be the concern of the Referee whether it occurs before, during, or after the event.

Part 5 outlines some of the tasks of the Referee and, when available, the Assistant Referees. It also includes a description of the method of match control employed by the officials – *The Diagonal System*.

Summarizing, an organized football match cannot be played to its full potential without the supervision of neutral officials. They apply the principles of the 'spirit of the game' by ensuring that each player has an *equal opportunity* to demonstrate skills, with concern for *safety* within the rules to aim for maximum *enjoyment*.

In football the decisions of the Referee, relating to facts connected with play, are **final** even when they may be seen to be in error. The best advice for any player in doubt is to 'Play to the Whistle'.

USUAL DRESS AND
EQUIPMENT

IN POCKET:

COIN

STOPWATCH

EXTRA WHISTLE

EXTRA PENCIL

PENCIL

NOTEBOOK

CARDS
(RED AND
YELLOW)

WHISTLE
ATTACHED
TO WRIST

WRIST WATCH

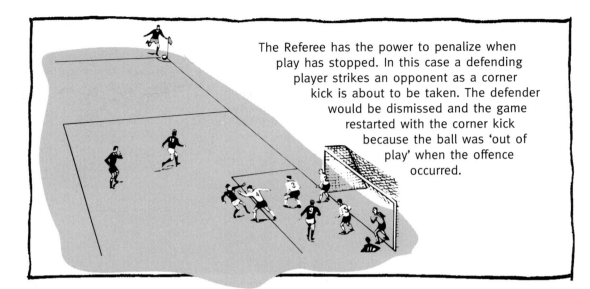

The Referee has the power to penalize when play has stopped. In this case a defending player strikes an opponent as a corner kick is about to be taken. The defender would be dismissed and the game restarted with the corner kick because the ball was 'out of play' when the offence occurred.

The attacking player (No.8) is fouled but the Referee has the power to refrain from stopping the play if it would be to the advantage of the offended team to continue. However, if the advantage is not realized within a few seconds the Referee can penalize the original offence.

A defending player attempts to prevent a goal being scored by deliberately handling the ball. If the ball enters the goal, the Referee will allow the goal and not award a penalty kick for the handling offence.

If the ball does not enter the goal the offending player is dismissed for denying opponents an obvious goal opportunity.

The Referee has the power to stop the game if, in his opinion, a player is seriously injured.

Any player bleeding from an injury must leave the field and will only be allowed to return when the bleeding has stopped.

No person, other than the players and Assistant Referees may enter the field of play without the Referee's permission. In the situation shown here the team official may be warned and reported.

To communicate the severity of a disciplinary sanction, to the player concerned and to others, the Referee produces a card:

Yellow card = Caution

Red card = Dismissal from the match

SIGNALS - BY THE REFEREE

By Law. Only two signals are mandatory in the Laws of the Game:
- INDIRECT FREE KICK –- one arm raised above the head
- DISCIPLINE CARDS – display of a coloured card to an offending player.

Approved signals. Instructions to players.

- PLAY ON ADVANTAGE – where the Referee observes an offence but decides to apply the advantage option and signals play to continue

- DIRECT FREE KICK – a hand and arm signal to indicate the direction of the free kick

- PENALTY KICK – pointing to the penalty mark

- OTHER APPROVED SIGNALS – pointing to the appropriate position for a throw in, goal kick, corner-kick, free kick.

PLAY ON ADVANTAGE

INDIRECT FREE KICK

DIRECT FREE KICK – DIRECTION

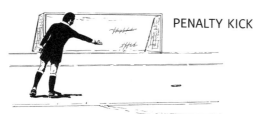

PENALTY KICK

HANDLING THE BALL

PUSHING

Informative (unofficial). Instinctive gestures communicating the nature of offences, e.g. handling the ball, pushing, etc.

Neutral Assistant Referees, when appointed, are selected from a panel of qualified Referees. As their title suggests they assist the Referee to control a match in accordance with his instructions and the Laws of the Game.

Here, an Assistant Referee reports an offence by an attacking player which he noticed immediately prior to the scoring of a goal. The Referee, if he has not observed the incident, may act on the advice and cancel the goal.

If the ball strikes an Assistant Referee and is deflected over a boundary line the game is restarted with a throw-in, goal kick or corner kick. In this case it would be a corner kick because a defending player last touched the ball and it was deflected over the goal line.

SIGNALS FOR THE INFORMATION OF THE REFEREE.
Flag signals indicate to the Referee when the ball goes out of play over a touch- or goal line and the correct decision e.g. a goal kick, corner kick, or which side is entitled to a throw-in.

A special signal draws the Referee's attention to a request for a substitution.

CORNER KICK

GOAL KICK

SUBSTITUTION

THROW-IN DIRECTION

Offside. A series of signals to indicate when a player, in an Offside Position, may be penalized and the position of the offence.

SIGNALS – OFFSIDE.

Flag in vertical position.

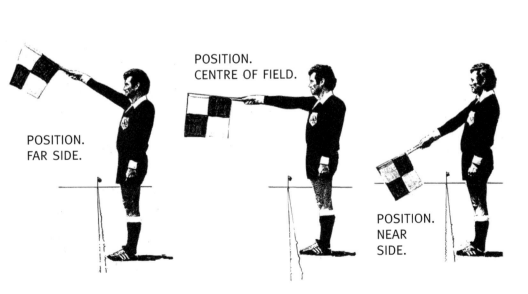

POSITION.
CENTRE OF FIELD.

POSITION.
FAR SIDE.

POSITION.
NEAR
SIDE.

THE DIAGONAL SYSTEM OF CONTROL FOR MATCH OFFICIALS

The imaginary diagonal used by the Referee is the line A-B.

The opposite diagonal, used by the Assistant Referees AR1 and AR2, is adjusted to the position of the Referee.

If the Referee is near A, AR2 will be at a point between M and K. When the Referee is at B, AR1 will be between E and F. This gives two officials control of the respective 'danger zones', one at each side of the field.

AR1 adopts the Reds as his side: AR2 adopts the Blues. As Red forwards move towards the Blue goal AR1 keeps up with their foremost man, so in actual practice, he will rarely get into the Reds' half of the field. Similarly, AR2 keeps up with the foremost blue player and will rarely get into the Blues' half.

At corner kicks or penalty kicks, the assistant, in that half where the corner kick or penalty kick occurs, positions himself at N, M or F, according to the Referee's instructions. The Referee then takes position.

The diagonal system fails if AR2 gets between G and H when the Referee is at B, or when AR1 is near C or D when the Referee is at A, because there are two officials in the same place. This should be avoided.

Note: Some Referees prefer to use the opposite diagonal, viz, from F to M, in which case the Assistants adjust their patrol accordingly.

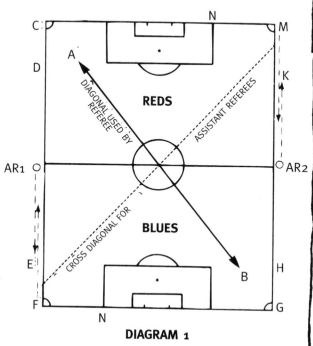

DIAGRAM 1

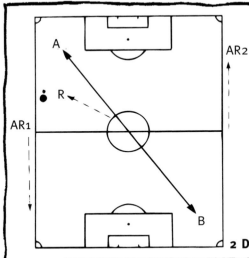

THE DIAGONAL SYSTEM OF CONTROL FOR MATCH OFFICIALS

Ball moves out to left wing. Referee (R) slightly off diagonal to be near play.

Assistant Referee (AR2) level with spearhead of attack.

Two officials, therefore, are level with spearhead of attack.

AR1 is in position for clearances and possible counter-attack.

2 DEVELOPMENT OF ATTACK

3 FREE KICK NEAR GOAL
(just outside the penalty area)

PLAYERS • AND ○
LINE UP FOR FREE KICK.

Referee (R) takes up his position just off his diagonal so that he is placed accurately to judge offside.

AR2 is more advanced but can watch for offside and fouls and is also in a good position to act as goal judge in the event of a direct shot being taken.

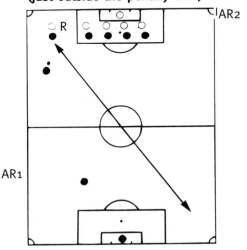

Part 6

HELP FOOTBALL

Guidelines for the football family:
'For the good of the game' (FIFA)

PLAYER

REFEREE

COACH

ORGANIZERS

SUPPORTERS

THE FIFA FAIR PLAY CAMPAIGN
'FOR THE GOOD OF THE GAME'

Code of conduct

Ten golden rules

1. play to win

2. play fair

3. observe the Laws of the Game

4. respect opponents, team-mates, Referees, officials and spectators

5. accept defeat with dignity

6. promote the interests of football

7. reject corruption, drugs, racism, violence and other dangers to our sport

8. help others to resist corrupting pressures

9. denounce those who attempt to discredit our sport

10. honour those who defend football's good reputation

GUIDELINES – PLAYER

You want to have fun and improve your game. Knowing something about the rules will add to your interest in football and help avoid problems on the field.

Equipment Before every game check your equipment for any item which may prove to be dangerous to yourself or opponents. Footwear, in particular the studs you choose to suit the field surface condition, needs special care. The Referee may ask you to remove items of jewellery.

Starting play Remember the ball is not in play until kicked. The signal for the kick is not the signal for you to move nearer than ten yards to the ball.

Ball out of play The whole of the ball must be over the boundary lines before it is out of play.

Free kick position Free kicks must be taken from the place where the offence occurred and the ball must be stationary when it is kicked.

Ten yards please Check what ten yards means, e.g. the centre circle has a ten-yard radius, and be at least this distance as soon as a free kick is awarded against your team. You will avoid a yellow card.

Offside It's very important to understand this rule because your team loses a chance to score, and the ball is given to the opposing team, every time you are caught offside. Study carefully the explanations and illustrations in Part 3. In particular realize that offside is, first, a matter of **fact**, i.e. your position in relation to the ball and opposing players, second, a matter of the **opinion of the Referee** as to your involvement in **active play** and any advantage you may gain by being in an **offside position.**

Offside position is judged at the **moment the ball touches, or is played by a team-mate, not where you are when you receive the ball.**

(a) You cannot be offside if you are **behind the ball.** If you are ahead of the ball be aware of the positions of opponents. Try to keep at least two between you and their goal line.

(b) If you are in an **offside position** either, get back behind the ball, or, avoid the **next area of active play** to convince the Referee that you are not influencing play or trying to gain an advantage.

(c) You cannot be offside if you receive the ball direct from a goal kick, a corner kick or a throw-in.

Unfair play You want to show your skills with the ball. So do opponents. Challenges for possession often involve hard physical contact. You will avoid being penalized if you control your challenges with care and without being reckless or using excessive force.

Charging an opponent You may charge an opponent fairly but not when the ball is not within playing distance or when you are making no attempt to play it.

Sporting behaviour Nobody enjoys the spectacle of a player being cautioned or sent off. Understand, from Law 12, what actions are unacceptable and can be avoided.

Penalty kicks The important points to remember are:

(a) the positions of the players,

(b) players must remain at proper distances until the ball is in play,

(c) the ball is in play when it is kicked forward.

Throw-in position Throw-ins must be taken from the point where the ball crossed the touch line.

Goalkeepers You *must* know the following:

(a) Wear colours which distinguish you from other players and the Referee.

(b) The rules are strict about the amount of time that you are allowed possession of the ball and when you must not touch it with your hands.

(c) When you take the ball into your hands you must release it into play without taking more than four steps or more than a few seconds. If you exceed about six seconds you risk giving the opponents a free kick in a very dangerous position.

(d) Avoid any tactics which may be interpreted as wasting time.

(e) When challenged for the ball avoid distracting opponents by shouting.

(f) You will be penalized if you touch the ball with your hands if a team-mate deliberately kicks it to you or throws it direct to you from a throw-in.

(g) Regarding item (c) understand that if you deliberately parry the ball with your hands you are still considered to be in possession. Release the ball without touching it again with your hands.

(h) When facing a penalty kick you may move *along* your goal line, before the ball is kicked, but not from it, e.g. advancing towards the ball. Also avoid any gestures which may be interpreted as attempts to distract the penalty-kicker. This is unsporting behaviour.

(i) If you intend changing places with a team-mate be sure to advise the Referee in advance.

GUIDELINES – REFEREE

You have a vital role to play with regard to the amount of pleasure people obtain from football.

Every game poses a variety of problems requiring instant and correct decisions. Only by clearly understanding the purpose and application of each Law can you carry out your duties efficiently. Some problems will arise which do not have written answers. These must be solved with the application of common sense. Your feeling for what is fair and unfair will guide you to the right decision.

For qualified Referees the following guidelines are intended as reminders of the basic duties and responsibilities you have been trained to accept.

For other members of the football family a glance at the guidelines will give an insight to the contribution of match officials to keep football a clean, healthy, and enjoyable family sport.

PART 1. COMPONENTS
Check list Establish a routine method of checking all components by making a list of items to be examined. Your list should include the following:

(a) **Field** – condition of the playing surface, line markings, dimensions, inside areas, penalty and centre marks, technical areas for coaches.

(b) **Goals** – safety of construction, anchorage, size, colour, nets.

(c) **Flag posts** – positions, height, safety of construction.

(d) **Ball** – shape, size, pressure to suit game conditions, conformity with FIFA standards where necessary. In a hot climate check the ball pressure at field temperature not dressing room temperature. Spare ball(s)?

(e) **Players** – number on each team, substitutes, names, goalkeepers.

(f) **Players' equipment** – colours, footwear, dangerous ornaments.

(g) **Coaches** – identity

(h) **Time** – complete checks to allow sufficient time to adjust incorrect items.

PART 2. RULES OF PLAY
COMPETITION RULES
Check for any additions to, or variations from, the Laws which have been agreed to between the competing teams. In particular:

(a) *Components* – for players under 16 years of age, women and veteran players.

(b) *Timing* – for players in item (a), periods of extra time.

Allow for time lost due to delays for substitutions, injuries, time-wasting tactics, any other cause at your discretion.

Players have a right to an interval at half-time not exceeding fifteen minutes.

(c) *Free kicks* – allow free kicks to be taken as quickly as possible so that the offending team do not gain an advantage by using delay to organize their defence.

    (i) The ball must be stationary before kick is taken.

    (ii) Caution any player attempting to delay a free kick, e.g. by moving the ball from its correct position.

    (iii) Caution any player of the offending team who refuses to retire to the proper distance before the kick is taken.

    (iv) At an indirect free kick raise one arm before the signal to take the kick.

(d) *Goals* – Do not award a goal unless you are sure that the ball has wholly crossed the goal line between the posts and under the crossbar.

    (i) Check with your Assistant Referees before awarding a goal.

      A goal cannot be cancelled after play has been restarted.

    (ii) Keep a record of each goal as it is scored.

PART 3. OFFSIDE

Basics

You have to decide, first, is the player in an offside position? This is not an offence until you make a second decision based on your judgement of the player's influence on the play.

(a) *Offside position* – Is the player in front of the ball in the opponents' half? If so, and he is nearer to the goal line than the second last opponent, the player is in an offside position.

(b) *Offside offence* – Is the player involved in the zone of play , e.g. by moving towards an opponent or the ball, or, gaining an advantage? If so, this is an offside offence.

(c) *Moment of assessment* – Offside decisions are assessed at the moment the ball touches, or is played, by a teammate.

Part 4 . FOULS AND MISCONDUCT

Foul play – Most foul play occurs when two players challenge for possession of the ball. Physical contact is inevitable in most instances and is an accepted part of the game. However, challenges must be kept under control and, to be fair, they must not be careless, reckless, or involve excessive force.

Dangerous play – Attempting to play the ball may, sometimes, put an opponent in danger, e.g. when the ball is close to the opponent's head or chest. An indirect free kick is the correct award.

Youth and women players – It is advisable to take special care, in matches with youth or women players, to interpret physical challenges on the side of caution in order to reduce the risk of injuries.

Misconduct – A policy of strict control over all forms of misconduct is recommended, not only to guide the particular match in your charge, but also to protect the overall image of the game. In particular:

(a) ***Unsporting behaviour*** – Attempts to gain an unfair advantage, contesting decisions, and disregard for the Laws of the Game, form the general character of *unsporting behaviour* in football. The purpose of cautioning players, for any act under this heading, is to reduce the need for more serious disciplinary action in subsequent play.

(b) ***Serious misconduct*** – Any player, who continues to behave in an unsporting manner after receiving a caution, who commits serious foul play, who behaves violently, who insults opponents or officials, or denies the opposing team a fair chance to score a goal, deserves the penalty of dismissal from a match and further punishment by the competent authorities.

(c) ***Prevention*** – A timely word of advice from you, to players who appear to be losing self-control, will help to complete the match without the necessity for severe disciplinary action.

PART 5. PLAY TO THE WHISTLE
Match control
You may, or may not, have the aid of assistant Referees to control your match. Whatever the situation give careful thought to pre-game conditions and how they may affect your method of control. You can form your opinion during the pre-game check of the components listed in Part 1.

(a) ***Advantage*** – You have a few seconds of reflection to decide if a decision to allow advantage will have the desired effect. Do not hesitate to call back the play if it does not work. Also, do not allow an offender to escape a caution, or dismissal (where appropriate) if it does work.

(b) ***Injured players*** – Stop the game immediately if a player appears to be seriously injured. You may save the player from long-term handicap, or worse. Do not wait for players to kick the ball out of play – it is your duty to act quickly, particularly when a player has a head injury.

(c) ***Medical assistance*** – Find out before the game where you can call for aid should it be needed promptly.

(d) ***Slight injuries*** – Wait for a normal stoppage to allow slightly injured players to leave the field for treatment. Where young or women players are involved it is advisable to err on the side of discretion and stop play if in doubt. Remember, any player with a bleeding wound must leave the field for attention.

(e) ***Simulated injuries*** – Be alert to players who pretend to be injured to gain an advantage, e.g. delay, or to have an opponent disciplined.

COACHING
A coach is allowed to issue instructions to players during a match provided that it is done in a responsible manner. The person delegated to coach should be identified to you before the start of play.

(a) ***Technical area*** – Check whether such an area exists at your match. If not, find out from the coaches where they will be located.

(b) **Conduct** – Be aware of any abuse of the coaching privilege and report any unsporting behaviour to the competent authority.

Illegal entry into the field
Do not allow officials or any other person into the field of play without your permission.

SIGNALS
The Laws do not specify any code of signals apart from the raising of one arm to signify an indire free kick. However, simple and discreet gestures, e.g. touching a hand to indicate handball, will he to communicate with players, and others, and possibly reduce dissent.

GUIDELINES – ASSISTANT REFEREES

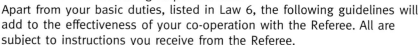

Neutral Officials – You are a fully qualified Referee appointed to a match as an Assistant Referee. Previous to 1996 your title was linesman. The new status recognized the importance of your task in assisting the match Referee with his increasing responsibilities.

Apart from your basic duties, listed in Law 6, the following guidelines will add to the effectiveness of your co-operation with the Referee. All are subject to instructions you receive from the Referee.

Components – Walk the field to check with the Referee. Bring to the Referee's notice any incorrect items.

Substitutes – Assist with the checking of names, where they are located, any special competition rules to be observed.

Timing of play – Time the play, as if you are the Referee. Does the Referee need a signal to indicat time remaining?

Off-the ball incidents – Any incidents of Serious Foul Play, Violent Conduct or any other misconduc which the Referee has not observed, must be notified without delay.

Offside – Know what the Referee wants in monitoring the play for offside situations, particularly at free kicks near the penalty area. Use field markings as references to judge zones of active play.

Coaching – Draw the Referee's attention to any misconduct or movement outside of the *technical area.*

Identification of offenders – Make a note of players disciplined for misconduct to ensure correct indentification in match reports.

Third team – The Referee and the two Assistant Referees form the 'third team' at a match. The degree of co-operation you achieve will have an important bearing on the efficiency of control and the enjoyment of play.

Club Assistant Referees
Fully qualified neutral Assistant Referees may not be available. The two teams in a match are require sometimes as a mandatory competition rule, to provide a person to act as a Club Assistant Referee.

Duties – Both Club Assistants must report to the Referee, before the start of the match, for instructions as to the manner in which they can co-operate in the conduct of the match.

General – The Referee usually asks for a signal to indicate that the ball has passed out of play over the touch line and which side is entitled to the throw-in. Other forms of assistance may be delegated but the Referee's decision is always final.

GUIDELINES – COACH

Your role in football was recognized in 1993 when the International Football Association Board agreed that you may convey tactical instructions to your players during the course of a match. This was an historio concession intended 'to add to the quality of play'. It was granted on two main conditions:

(a) that you give your instructions from a specific location, a *Technical Area* where this can be provided, and,

(b) that you behave in a responsible manner.

As only one person is allowed to issue instructions it is necessary that you identify yourself to the Referee before the start of the match.

After giving instructions you are required to return to your position.

If a formally marked *Technical Area* is not provided advise the Referee of the specific location from where you wish to give instructions. You should remain in that location.

You are usually a person with a great deal of experience in football and have in your charge young players whose characters are forming at an impressionable age. Apart from the technical guidance you are qualified to give, you are a strong influence on the degree of respect your players show for fair play, their attitudes towards opponents, match officials and spectators.

During a match you are as emotionally involved as the players because you want to obtain a good result. However, in granting the concession of coaching during the the play, the International Football Association Board expect you to accept the same criteria for correct behaviour as is required of the players.

GUIDELINES – ORGANIZERS

You may be a team manager, club official, competition organizer or a volunteer giving your time so that others may share your affection for football.

For the correct organization of each match the club has several duties and responsibilities. The following notes outline the main points.

Competitions – Clubs agree to comply with the rules of competitions which may vary in some respects with the Laws of the Game e.g. number of substitutes, periods of play, extra time, etc. It is the duty of the club to know both the Laws and agreed variations.

Match officials – The club in charge of match arrangements is responsible for the welfare of the match officials before, during, and after the match.

Club discipline – Each club is responsible for the proper conduct of its players and officials.

Match arrangements – The club in charge is responsible for providing:
- a field of play, correctly marked in accordance with Law 1, together with proper goals and cornerposts and flags. Goal nets are desirable but not compulsory.
- the match ball plus spare balls if possible.
- suitable dressing and washing facilities for the players and match officials.
- whenever possible, a suitable barrier between the playing field and spectators.
- sufficient space to be allowed to avoid interference with play and the patrol of assistant Referees.
- the match officials with full details of match location, time of kick-off and any other relevant information.

Consultation – Consult with the Referee on any matter which may affect the correct conduct of a match, e.g. security when many spectators are expected.

GUIDELINES – SUPPORTERS

You probably support a particular club and enjoy the football family atmosphere as you marvel at the skills of your favourite players. Your presence and encouragement stimulates players to play well.

You can help football in other ways to continue its attraction to sports people. Here are some suggestions:

Fair Play – Insist on fair play, not only from players of other teams but also from your own favourites.

Match Officials – Appreciate the task of the officials from the guidelines in this publication.They try to ensure that each match is played to the spirit as well as the letter of the rules. They are members of the football family and deserve your support.

Players' skills – Exciting skills are part of the joy of football, whether shown by your own players or opponents. Applaud both.

Combat negative influences – The FIFA Campaign for Fair Play appeals to the whole football family to recognize and combat dangers to football. Support FIFA by denouncing anyone who discredits our sport by corruption, drugs, racism or violence.

Other Supporters – Those who support opposing teams share your passion for the game. They, too, are members of the football family. Respect and salute them.

TO ALL SUPPORTERS! Help keep football a clean, healthy, and exciting sport, deserving of the title: **The People's Game.**

Part 7

THE OFFICIAL LAWS OF ASSOCIATION FOOTBALL

<u>Only seventeen</u> plus Decisions of the
International Football Association Board

Reproduction of the Laws of the Game and Decisions of the
International Football Association Board authorized by FIFA.

All rights reserved by FIFA

With grateful acknowledgements to FIFA for permission to reproduce the
Laws of the Game and other FIFA-related material.

NOTES ON THE LAWS OF THE GAME

MODIFICATIONS

Subject to the agreement of the national association concerned and provided the principles of
these Laws are maintained, the Laws may be modified in their application for matches for
players of under 16 years of age, for women footballers and for veteran footballers (over 35
years).

Any or all of the following modifications are permissible:
- size of the field of play
- size, weight and material of ball
- width between the goalposts and height of the crossbar from the ground
- the duration of the periods of play
- substitutions

Further modifications are only allowed with the consent of the International Football
Association Board.

MALE AND FEMALE

References to the male gender in the Laws of the Game in respect of Referees, Assistant
Referees, players and officials are for simplification and apply to both males and females.

KEY

Throughout the Laws of the Game the following symbol is used:
*Unless covered by the Special Circumstances listed in Law 8 — The Start and Restart of Play

CONTENTS

LAWS OF THE GAME

LAW 1 – THE FIELD OF PLAY

DIMENSIONS

The field of play must be rectangular. The length of the touch line must be greater than the length of the goal line.

Length: minimum 90 m (100 yds)   maximum 120 m (130 yds)
Width: minimum 45 m (50 yds)   maximum 90 m (100 yds)

International Matches
Length: minimum 100 m (110 yds)   maximum 110 m (120 yds)
Width: minimum 64 m (70 yds)   maximum 75 m (80 yds)

FIELD MARKINGS

The field of play is marked with lines. These lines belong to the areas of which they are boundaries.

The two longer boundary lines are called touch lines. The two shorter lines are called goal lines.

All lines are not more than 12 cm (5 ins) wide.

The field of play is divided into two halves by a halfway line.

The centre mark is indicated at the midpoint of the halfway line. A circle with a radius of 9.15 m (10 yds) is marked around it.

THE GOAL AREA

A goal area is defined at each end of the field as follows:

Two lines are drawn at right angles to the goal line, 5.5 m (6 yds) from the inside of each goalpost. These lines extend into the field of play for a distance of 5.5 m (6 yds) and are joined by a line drawn parallel with the goal line. The area bounded by these lines and the goal line is the goal area.

THE PENALTY AREA

A penalty area is defined at each end of the field as follows:

Two lines are drawn at right angles to the goal line, 16.5 m (18 yds) from the inside of each goalpost. These lines extend into the field of play for a distance of 16.5 m, (18 yds) and are joined by a line drawn parallel with the goal line. The area bounded by these lines and the goal line is the penalty area.
Within each penalty area a penalty mark is made 11 m (12 yds) from the midpoint between the goalposts and equidistant to them. An arc of a circle with a radius of 9.15 m (10 yds) from each penalty mark is drawn outside the penalty area.

FLAGPOSTS

A flagpost, not less than 1.5 m (5 ft) high, with a non-pointed top and a flag is placed at each corner.

Flagposts may also be placed at each end of the halfway line, not less than 1 m (1 yd) outside the touch line.

THE CORNER ARC

A quarter circle with a radius of 1 m (1 yd) from each corner flagpost is drawn inside the field of play.

GOALS

Goals must be placed on the centre of each goal line.

They consist of two upright posts equidistant from the corner flagposts and joined at the top by a horizontal crossbar.

The distance between the posts is 7.32 m (8 yds) and the distance from the lower edge of the crossbar to the ground is 2.44 m (8 ft).

Both goalposts and the crossbar have the same width and depth which do not exceed 12 cm (5 ins). The goal lines are the same width as that of the goalposts and the crossbar. Nets may be attached to the goals and the ground behind the goal, provided that they are properly supported and do not interfere with the goalkeeper.

The goalposts and crossbars must be white.

SAFETY

Goals must be anchored securely to the ground. Portable goals may only be used if they satisfy this requirement.

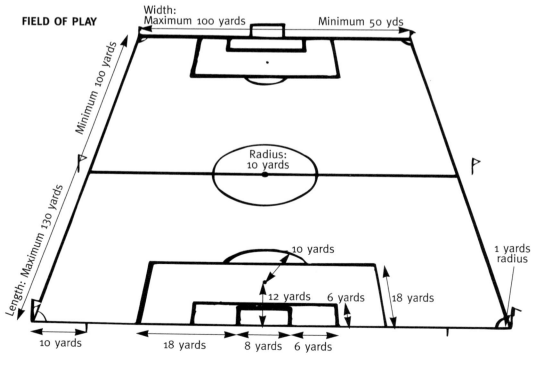

FIELD OF PLAY

Width: Maximum 100 yards   Minimum 50 yds

Minimum 100 yards

Length: Maximum 130 yards

Radius: 10 yards

1 yards radius

10 yards

12 yards   6 yards   18 yards

10 yards   18 yards   8 yards   6 yards

DECISIONS OF THE INTERNATIONAL F.A. BOARD

• DECISION 1
If the crossbar becomes displaced or broken, play is stopped until it has been repaired or replaced in position. If a repair is not possible, the match is abandoned. The use of a rope to replace the crossbar is not permitted. If the crossbar can be repaired, the match is restarted with a dropped ball at the place where the ball was located when play was stopped.*

• DECISION 2
Goalposts and crossbars must be made of wood, metal or other approved material. Their shape may be square, rectangular, round or elliptical and they must not be dangerous to players.

• DECISION 3
No kind of commercial advertising, whether real or virtual, is permitted on the field of play and field equipment (including the goal nets and the areas they enclose) from the time the teams enter the field of play until they have left it at half-time and from the time the teams re-enter the field of play until the end of the match. In particular, no advertising material of any kind may be displayed on goals, nets, flagposts or their flags. No extraneous equipment (cameras, microphones, etc.) may be attached to these items.

• DECISION 4
The reproduction, whether real or virtual, of representative logos or emblems of FIFA, confederations, national associations, leagues, clubs or other bodies, is forbidden on the field of play and field equipment (including the goal nets and the areas they enclose) during playing time, as described in Decision 3.

• DECISION 5
A mark may be made off the field of play, 9.15 metres (10 yds) from the corner arc and at right angles to the goal lines to ensure that this distance is observed when a corner kick is being taken.

LAW 2 – THE BALL

QUALITIES AND MEASUREMENTS
The ball is:
- spherical
- made of leather or other suitable material
- of a circumference of not more than 70cm (28 ins) and not less than 68cm (27 ins,)
- not more than 450g (16 oz) in weight and not less than 410g (14 oz) at the start of the match
- of a pressure equal to 0.6 — 1.1 atmosphere (600 —1100g/cm2) at sea level (8.5 lbs/sq in 15.6 lbs/sq in)

REPLACEMENT OF A DEFECTIVE BALL
If the ball bursts or becomes defective during the course of a match:
- the match is stopped
- the match is restarted by dropping the replacement ball at the place where the first ball became defective*

If the ball bursts or becomes defective whilst not in play at a kick-off, goal kick, corner kick, free kick, penalty kick or throw-in:
- the match is restarted accordingly

The ball may not be changed during the match without the authority of the Referee.

DECISIONS OF THE INTERNATIONAL F.A. BOARD

• DECISION 1

In competition matches, only footballs which meet the minimum technical requirements stipulated in Law 2 are permitted for use.

In FIFA competition matches, and in competition matches organized under the auspices of the confederations, acceptance of a football for use is conditional upon the football bearing one of the following three designations:

the official 'FIFA APPROVED' logo,   or
the official 'FIFA INSPECTED' logo,   or
the reference 'INTERNATIONAL MATCHBALL STANDARD'

Such a designation on a football indicates that it has been tested officially and found to be in compliance with specific technical requirements, different for each category and additional to the minimum specifications stipulated in Law 2. The list of the additional requirements specific to each of the respective categories must be approved by the International F. A. Board. The institutes conducting the tests are subject to the approval of FIFA.

National association competitions may require the use of balls bearing any one of these three designations.

In all other matches the ball used must satisfy the requirements of Law 2.

• DECISION 2

In FIFA competition matches and in competition matches organized under the auspices of the confederations and national associations, no kind of commercial advertising on the ball is permitted, except for the emblem of the competition, the competition organizer and the authorized trademark of the manufacturer. The competition regulations may restrict the size and number of such markings.

INTERNATIONAL MATCHBALL STANDARD

LAW 3 – THE NUMBER OF PLAYERS

PLAYERS
A match is played by two teams, each consisting of not more than eleven players, one of whom is the goalkeeper. A match may not start if either team consists of fewer than seven players.

OFFICIAL COMPETITIONS
Up to a maximum of three substitutes may be used in any match played in an official competition organized under the auspices of FIFA, the confederations or the national associations.

The rules of the competition must state how many substitutes may be nominated, from three up to a maximum of seven.

OTHER MATCHES
In other matches, up to five substitutes may be used, provided that:
• the teams concerned reach agreement on a maximum number
• the Referee is informed before the match

If the Referee is not informed, or if no agreement is reached before the start of the match, no more than three substitutes are allowed.

ALL MATCHES
In all matches the names of the substitutes must be given to the Referee prior to the start of the match. Substitutes not so named may not take part in the match.

SUBSTITUTION PROCEDURE
To replace a player by a substitute, the following conditions must be observed:
• the Referee is informed before any proposed substitution is made
• a substitute only enters the field of play after the player being replaced has left and after receiving a signal from the Referee
• a substitute only enters the field of play at the halfway line and during a stoppage in the match
• a substitution is completed when a substitute enters the field of play
• from that moment, the substitute becomes a player and the player he has replaced ceases to be a player
• a player who has been replaced takes no further part in the match
• all substitutes are subject to the authority and jurisdiction of the Referee, whether called upon to play or not

CHANGING THE GOALKEEPER
Any of the other players may change places with the goalkeeper, provided that:
• the Referee is informed before the change is made
• the change is made during a stoppage in the match

INFRINGEMENTS/SANCTIONS

If a substitute enters the field of play without the Referee's permission:

- play is stopped
- the substitute is cautioned, shown the yellow card and required to leave the field of play
- play is restarted with a dropped ball at the place it was located when play was stopped*

If a player changes places with the goalkeeper without the Referee's permission before the change is made:

- play continues
- the players concerned are cautioned and shown the yellow card when the ball is next out of play

For any other infringements of this Law:

- the players concerned are cautioned and shown the yellow card

RESTART OF PLAY

If play is stopped by the Referee to administer a caution:

- the match is restarted by an indirect free kick, to be taken by a player of the opposing team from the place where the ball was located when play was stopped*

PLAYERS AND SUBSTITUTES SENT OFF

A player who has been sent off before the kick-off may be replaced only by one of the named substitutes.

A named substitute who has been sent off, either before the kick-off or after play has started, may not be replaced.

DECISIONS OF THE INTERNATIONAL F.A. BOARD

- ## DECISION 1
Subject to the overriding conditions of Law 3, the minimum number of players in a team is left to the discretion of national associations. The Board is of the opinion, however, that a match should not continue if there are fewer than seven players in either team.

- ## DECISION 2
The coach may convey tactical instructions to the players during the match. He and the other officials must remain within the confines of the technical area, where such an area is provided, and they must behave in a responsible manner.

LAW 4 – THE PLAYERS' EQUIPMENT

SAFETY

A player must not use equipment or wear anything which is dangerous to himself or another player (including any kind of jewellery).

BASIC EQUIPMENT

The basic compulsory equipment of a player is:

- a jersey or shirt
- shorts — if thermal undershorts are worn, they are of the same main colour as the shorts
- stockings
- shinguards
- footwear

SHINGUARDS

- are covered entirely by the stockings
- are made of a suitable material (rubber, plastic, or similar substances)
- provide a reasonable degree of protection

GOALKEEPERS

- each goalkeeper wears colours which distinguish him from the other players, the Referee and the Assistant Referees

INFRINGEMENTS/SANCTIONS

For any infringement of this Law:

- play need not be stopped
- the player at fault is instructed by the Referee to leave the field of play to correct his equipment
- the player leaves the field of play when the ball next ceases to be in play unless he has already corrected his equipment
- any player required to leave the field of play to correct his equipment does not re-enter without the Referee's permission
- the Referee checks that the player's equipment is correct before allowing him to re-enter the field of play
- the player is only allowed to re-enter the field of play when the ball is out of play

A player who has been required to leave the field of play because of an infringement of this Law and who enters (or re-enters) the field of play without the Referee's permission is cautioned and shown the yellow card.

RESTART OF PLAY

If play is stopped by the Referee to administer a caution:

- the match is restarted by an indirect free kick taken by an player of the opposing side from the place where the ball was located when the Referee stopped the match*

LAW 5 – THE REFEREE

THE AUTHORITY OF THE REFEREE

Each match is controlled by a Referee who has full authority to enforce:the Laws of the Game in connection with the match to which he has been appointed.

POWERS AND DUTIES

THE REFEREE:
- enforces the Laws of the Game
- controls the match in co-operation with the Assistant Referees and, where applicable, with the Fourth Official
- ensures that any ball used meets with the requirements of Law 2
- ensures that players' equipment meets the requirements of Law 4
- acts as timekeeper and keeps a record of the match
- stops, suspends or terminates the match, at his discretion, for any infringements of the Laws
- stops, suspends or terminates the match because of outside interference of any kind
- stops the match if, in his opinion, a player is seriously injured and ensures that he is removed from the field of play
- allows play to continue until the ball is out of play if a player is, in his opinion, only slightly injured
- ensures that any player bleeding from a wound leaves the field of play. The player may only return on receiving a signal from the Referee, who must be satisfied that the bleeding has stopped
- allows play to continue when the team against which an offence has been committed will benefit from such an advantage and penalizes the original offence if the anticipated advantage does not ensue at that time
- punishes the more serious offence when a player commits more than one offence at the same time
- takes disciplinary action against players guilty of cautionable and sending-off offences. He is not obliged to take this action immediately but must do so when the ball next goes out of play
- takes action against team officials who fail to conduct themselves in a responsible manner and may at his discretion, expel them from the field of play and its immediate surrounds
- acts on the advice of Assistant Referees regarding incidents which he has not seen
- ensures that no unauthorized persons enter the field of play
- restarts the match after it has been stopped
- provides the appropriate authorities with a match report which includes information on any disciplinary action taken against players, and/or team officials and any other incidents which occurred before, during or after the match

DECISIONS OF THE REFEREE

The decisions of the Referee regarding facts connected with play are final.
The Referee may only change a decision on realizing that it is incorrect or, at his discretion, on the advice of an Assistant Referee, provided that he has not restarted play.

DECISIONS OF THE INTERNATIONAL F.A. BOARD

• **DECISION 1**

A Referee (or where applicable, an Assistant Referee or Fourth Official) is not held liable for:

any kind of injury suffered by a player, official or spectator

any damage to property of any kind

any other loss suffered by any individual, club, company, association or other body, which is due or which may be due to any decision which he may take under the terms of the Laws of the Game or in respect of the normal procedures required to hold, play and control a match.

This may include:
- a decision that the condition of the field of play or its surrounds or that the weather conditions are such as to allow or not to allow a match to take place
- a decision to abandon a match for whatever reason
- a decision as to the condition of the fixtures or equipment used during a match including the goalposts, crossbar, flagposts and the ball
- a decision to stop or not to stop a match due to spectator interference or any problem in the spectator area
- a decision to stop or not to stop play to allow an injured player to be removed from the field of play for treatment
- a decision to request or insist that an injured player be removed from the field of play for treatment
- a decision to allow or not to allow a player to wear certain apparel or equipment
- a decision (in so far as this may be his responsibility) to allow or not to allow any persons (including team or stadium officials, security officers, photographers or other media representatives) to be present in the vicinity of the field of play
- any other decision which he may take in accordance with the Laws of the Game or in conformity with his duties under the terms of FIFA, confederation, national association or league rules or regulations under which the match is played

• **DECISION 2**

In tournaments or competitions where a Fourth Official is appointed, his role and duties must be in accordance with the guidelines approved by the International F.A. Board.

• **DECISION 3**

Facts connected with play shall include whether a goal is scored or not and the result of the match.

LAW 6 – THE ASSISTANT REFEREES

DUTIES
Two Assistant Referees are appointed whose duties, subject to the decision of the Referee, are to indicate:
- when the whole of the ball has passed out of the field of play
- which side is entitled to a corner kick, goal kick or throw-in
- when a player may be penalized for being in an offside position
- when a substitution is requested
- when misconduct or any other incident has occurred out of the view of the Referee

ASSISTANCE
The Assistant Referees also assist the Referee to control the match in accordance with the Laws of the Game.

In the event of undue interference or improper conduct, the Referee will relieve an Assistant Referee of his duties and make a report to the appropriate authorities.

LAW 7 – THE DURATION OF THE MATCH

PERIODS OF PLAY
The match lasts two equal periods of 45 minutes, unless otherwise mutually agreed between the Referee and the two participating teams. Any agreement to alter the periods of play (for example to reduce each half to 40 minutes because of insufficient light) must be made before the start of play and must comply with competition rules.

HALF-TIME INTERVAL
Players are entitled to an interval at half-time.

The half-time interval must not exceed 15 minutes.

Competition rules must state the duration of the half-time interval.

The duration of the half-time interval may be altered only with the consent of the Referee.

ALLOWANCE FOR TIME LOST
Allowance is made in either period for all time lost through:
- substitution(s)
- assessment of injury to players
- removal of injured players from the field of play for treatment
- wasting time
- any other cause

The allowance for time lost is at the discretion of the Referee.

PENALTY KICK
Additional time is allowed for a penalty kick to be taken at the end of each half or at the end of periods of extra time.

EXTRA TIME
Competition rules may provide for two further equal periods to be played. The conditions of Law 8 will apply.

ABANDONED MATCH
An abandoned match is replayed unless the competition rules provide otherwise.

LAW 8 – THE START AND RESTART OF PLAY

PRELIMINARIES
A coin is tossed and the team which wins the toss decides which goal it will attack in the first half of the match.

The other team takes the kick-off to start the match.

The team which wins the toss takes the kick-off to start the second half of the match.

In the second half of the match the teams change ends and attack the opposite goals.

KICK-OFF
A kick-off is a way of starting or restarting play:
- at the start of the match
- after a goal has been scored
- at the start of the second half of the match
- at the start of each period of extra time, where applicable

A goal may be scored directly from the kick-off.

PROCEDURE
- all players are in their own half of the field
- the opponents of the team taking the kick-off are at least 9.15 m (10 yds) from the ball until it is in play
- the ball is stationary on the centre mark
- the Referee gives a signal
- the ball is in play when it is kicked and moves forward
- the kicker does not touch the ball a second time until it has touched another player

After a team scores a goal, the kick-off is taken by the other team.

INFRINGEMENTS/SANCTIONS

If the kicker touches the ball a second time before it has touched another player:
• an indirect free kick is awarded to the opposing team to be taken from the place where the infringement occurred*

For any other infringement of the kick-off procedure:
• the kick-off is retaken

DROPPED BALL

A dropped ball is a way of restarting the match after a temporary stoppage which becomes necessary, while the ball is in play, for any reason not mentioned elsewhere in the Laws of the Game.

PROCEDURE

The Referee drops the ball at the place where it was located when play was stopped.*

Play restarts when the ball touches the ground.

INFRINGEMENTS/SANCTIONS

The ball is dropped again:
• if it is touched by a player before it makes contact with the ground
• if the ball leaves the field of play after it makes contact with the ground without a player touching it

SPECIAL CIRCUMSTANCES

A free kick awarded to the defending team inside its own goal area is taken from any point within the goal area.

An indirect free kick awarded to the attacking team in its opponents' goal area is taken from the goal area line parallel to the goal line at the point nearest to where the infringement occurred.

A dropped ball to restart the match after play has been temporarily stopped inside the goal area takes place on the goal area line parallel to the goal line at the point nearest to where the ball was located when play was stopped.

LAW 9 – THE BALL IN AND OUT OF PLAY

BALL OUT OF PLAY

The ball is out of play when:
• it has wholly crossed the goal line or touch line, whether on the ground or in the air
• play has been stopped by the Referee

BALL IN PLAY

The ball is in play at all other times, including when:
• it rebounds from a goalpost, crossbar or corner flagpost and remains in the field of play
• it rebounds from either the Referee or an Assistant Referee when they are on the field of play

LAW 10 – THE METHOD OF SCORING

GOAL SCORED

A goal is scored when the whole of the ball passes over the goal line, between the goalposts and under the crossbar, provided that no infringement of the Laws of the Game has been committed previously by the team scoring the goal.

WINNING TEAM

The team scoring the greater number of goals during a match is the winner. If both teams score an equal number of goals, or if no goals are scored, the match is drawn.

COMPETITION RULES

For matches ending in a draw, competition rules may state provisions involving extra time, or other procedures approved by the International F.A. Board to determine the winner of a match.

LAW 11 – OFFSIDE

OFFSIDE POSITION

It is not an offence in itself to be in an offside position.

A player is in an offside position if:
• he is nearer to his opponents' goal line than both the ball and the second last opponent

A player is not in an offside position if:
• he is in his own half of the field of play   or
• he is level with the second last opponent   or
• he is level with the last two opponents

OFFENCE

A player in an offside position is only penalized if, at the moment the ball touches or is played by one of his team, he is, in the opinion of the Referee, involved in active play by:
• interfering with play   or
• interfering with an opponent   or
• gaining an advantage by being in that position

NO OFFENCE

There is no offside offence if a player receives the ball directly from:
• a goal kick   or
• a throw-in   or
• a corner kick

INFRINGEMENTS/SANCTIONS

For any offside offence, the Referee awards an indirect free kick to the opposing team to be taken from the place where the infringement occurred.*

LAW 12 – FOULS AND MISCONDUCT

Fouls and misconduct are penalized as follows:

DIRECT FREE KICK

A direct free kick is awarded to the opposing team if a player commits any of the following six offences in a manner considered by the Referee to be careless, reckless or using excessive force:
- kicks or attempts to kick an opponent
- trips or attempts to trip an opponent
- jumps at an opponent
- charges an opponent
- strikes or attempts to strike an opponent
- pushes an opponent

A direct free kick is also awarded to the opposing team if a player commits any of the following four offences:
- tackles an opponent to gain possession of the ball, making contact with the opponent before touching the ball
- holds an opponent
- spits at an opponent
- handles the ball deliberately (except for the goalkeeper within his own penalty area)

A direct free kick is taken from where the offence occurred.*

PENALTY KICK

A penalty kick is awarded if any of the above ten offences is committed by a player inside his own penalty area, irrespective of the position of the ball, provided it is in play.

INDIRECT FREE KICK

An indirect free kick is awarded to the opposing team if a goalkeeper, inside his own penalty area, commits any of the following five offences:
- takes more than four steps while controlling the ball with his hands, before releasing it from his possession
- touches the ball again with his hands after it has been released from his possession and has not touched any other player
- touches the ball with his hands after it has been deliberately kicked to him by a team-mate
- touches the ball with his hands after he has received it directly from a throw-in taken by a team-mate
- wastes time

An indirect free kick is also awarded to the opposing team if a player, in the opinion of the Referee:
- plays in a dangerous manner
- impedes the progress of an opponent
- prevents the goalkeeper from releasing the ball from his hands

- commits any other offence, not previously mentioned in Law 12, for which play is stopped to caution or dismiss a player

The indirect free kick is taken from where the offence occurred.*

DISCIPLINARY SANCTIONS
CAUTIONABLE OFFENCES
A player is cautioned and shown the yellow card if he commits any of the following seven offences:
1. is guilty of unsporting behaviour
2. shows dissent by word or action
3. persistently infringes the Laws of the Game
4. delays the restart of play
5. fails to respect the required distance when play is restarted with a corner kick or free kick
6. enters or re-enters the field of play without the Referee's permission
7. deliberately leaves the field of play without the Referee's permission

SENDING-OFF OFFENCES
A player is sent off and shown the red card if he commits any of the following seven offences:
1. is guilty of serious foul play
2. is guilty of violent conduct
3. spits at an opponent or any other person
4. denies the opposing team a goal or an obvious goal-scoring opportunity by deliberately handling the ball (this does not apply to a goalkeeper within his own penalty area)
5. denies an obvious goal-scoring opportunity to an opponent moving towards the player's goal by an offence punishable by a free kick or a penalty kick
6. uses offensive, insulting or abusive language
7. receives a second caution in the same match

DECISIONS OF THE INTERNATIONAL F.A. BOARD

- **DECISION 1**

A penalty kick is awarded if, while the ball is in play, the goalkeeper, inside his own penalty area, strikes or attempts to strike an opponent by throwing the ball at him.

- **DECISION 2**

A player who commits a cautionable or sending-off offence, either on or off the field of play, whether directed towards an opponent, a team-mate, the Referee, an Assistant Referee or any other person, is disciplined according to the nature of the offence committed.

- **DECISION 3**

The goalkeeper is considered to be in control of the ball by touching it with any part of his hand or arms. Possession of the ball includes the goalkeeper deliberately parrying the ball, but does not include the circumstances where, in the opinion of the Referee, the ball rebounds accidentally from the goalkeeper, for example after he has made a save.

The goalkeeper is considered to be guilty of time-wasting if he holds the ball in his hands or arms for more than 5-6 seconds.

- **DECISION 4**

Subject to the terms of Law 12, a player may pass the ball to his own goalkeeper using his head or chest or knee, etc. If, however, in the opinion of the Referee, a player uses a deliberate trick while the ball is in play in order to circumvent the Law, the player is guilty of unsporting behaviour. He is cautioned, shown the yellow card and an indirect free kick is awarded to the opposing team from the place where the infringement occurred.*

A player using a deliberate trick to circumvent the Law while he is taking a free kick, is cautioned for unsporting behaviour and shown the yellow card. The free kick is retaken.

In such circumstances, it is irrelevant whether the goalkeeper subsequently touches the ball with his hands or not. The offence is committed by the player in attempting to circumvent both the letter and the spirit of Law 12.

- **DECISION 5**

A tackle from behind, which endangers the safety of an opponent, must be sanctioned as serious foul play.

- **DECISION 6**

Any simulating actions anywhere on the field, which are intended to deceive the Referee, must be sanctioned as unsporting behaviour.

LAW 13 – FREE KICKS

TYPES OF FREE KICKS
Free kicks are either direct or indirect.

For both direct and indirect free kicks, the ball must be stationary when the kick is taken and the kicker does not touch the ball a second time until it has touched another player.

THE DIRECT FREE KICK
- if a direct free kick is kicked directly into the opponents' goal, a goal is awarded
- if a direct free kick is kicked directly into the team's own goal, a corner kick is awarded to the opposing team

THE INDIRECT FREE KICK
SIGNAL
The Referee indicates an indirect free kick by raising his arm above his head. He maintains his arm in that position until the kick has been taken and the ball has touched another player or goes out of play.

BALL ENTERS THE GOAL
A goal can be scored only if the ball subsequently touches another player before it enters the goal.
- if an indirect free kick is kicked directly into the opponents' goal, a goal kick is awarded
- if an indirect free kick is kicked directly into the team's own goal, a corner kick is awarded to the opposing team

POSITION OF FREE KICK
FREE KICK INSIDE THE PENALTY AREA

Direct or indirect free kick to the defending team:
- all opponents are at least 9.15 (10 yds.) from the ball
- all opponents remain outside the penalty area until the ball is in play
- the ball is in play when it is kicked directly beyond the penalty area
- a free kick awarded in the goal area is taken from any point inside that area

Indirect free kick to the attacking team:
- all opponents are at least 9.15 m (10 yds) from the ball until it is in play, unless they are on their a own goal line between the goalposts
- the ball is in play when it is kicked and moves
- an indirect free kick awarded inside the goal area is taken from that part of the goal area line which runs parallel to the goal line, at the point nearest to where the infringement occurred

FREE KICK OUTSIDE THE PENALTY AREA

- all opponents are at least 9.15 m (10 yds) from the ball until it is in play
- the ball is in play when it is kicked and moves
- the free kick is taken from the place where the infringement occurred

INFRINGEMENTS/SANCTIONS

If, when a free kick is taken, an opponent is closer to the ball than the required distance:
- the kick is retaken

If, when a free kick is taken by the defending team from inside its own penalty area, the ball is not kicked directly into play:
- the kick is retaken

FREE KICK TAKEN BY A PLAYER OTHER THAN THE GOALKEEPER

If, after the ball is in play, the kicker touches the ball a second time (except with his hands) before it has touched another player:
- an indirect free kick is awarded to the opposing team, the kick to be taken from the place where the infringement occurred*

If, after the ball is in play, the kicker deliberately handles the ball before it has touched another player:
- a direct free kick is awarded to the opposing team, the kick to be taken from the place where the infringement occurred*
- a penalty kick is awarded if the infringement occurred inside the kicker's penalty area

FREE KICK TAKEN BY THE GOALKEEPER

If, after the ball is in play, the goalkeeper touches the ball a second time (except with his hands), before it has touched another player:
- an indirect free kick is awarded to the opposing team, the kick to be taken from the place where the infringement occurred*

If, after the ball is in play, the goalkeeper deliberately handles the ball before it has touched another player:
- a direct free kick is awarded to the opposing team if the infringement occurred outside the goalkeeper's penalty area, the kick to be taken from the place where the infringement occurred*
- an indirect free kick is awarded to the opposing team if the infringement occurred inside the goalkeeper's penalty area, the kick to be taken from the place where the infringement occurred*

LAW 14 – THE PENALTY KICK

A penalty kick is awarded against a team which commits one of the ten offences for which a direct free kick is awarded, inside its own penalty area and while the ball is in play.

A goal may be scored directly from a penalty kick.

Additional time is allowed for a penalty kick to be taken at the end of each half or at the end of periods of extra time.

POSITION OF THE BALL AND THE PLAYERS

The ball:
• is placed on the penalty mark

The player taking the penalty kick:
• is properly identified

The defending goalkeeper:
• remains on his goal line, facing the kicker, between the goalposts until the ball has been kicked

The players other than the kicker are located:
• inside the field of play
• outside the penalty area
• behind the penalty mark
• at least 9.15 m (10 yds) from the penalty mark

THE REFEREE

• does not signal for a penalty kick to be taken until the players have taken up position in accordance with the Law
• decides when a penalty kick has been completed

PROCEDURE

• the player taking the penalty kicks the ball forward
• he does not play the ball a second time until it has touched another player
• the ball is in play when it is kicked and moves forward

When a penalty kick is taken during the normal course of play, or time has been extended at half-time or full time to allow a penalty kick to be taken or retaken, a goal is awarded if, before passing between the goalposts and under the crossbar:
• the ball touches either or both of the goalposts and/or the crossbar, and/or the goalkeeper

INFRINGEMENTS/SANCTIONS

IF THE REFEREE GIVES THE SIGNAL FOR A PENALTY KICK TO BE TAKEN AND, BEFORE THE BALL IS IN PLAY, ONE OF THE FOLLOWING SITUATIONS OCCURS:

The player taking the penalty kick infringes the Laws of the Game:
• the Referee allows the kick to proceed
• if the ball enters the goal, the kick is retaken
• if the ball does not enter the goal, the kick is not retaken

The goalkeeper infringes the Laws of the Game:
• the Referee allows the kick to proceed
• if the ball enters the goal, a goal is awarded
• if the ball does not enter the goal, the kick is retaken

A team-mate of the player taking the kick enters the penalty area or moves in front of or within 9.15 m (10 yds) of the penalty mark:

- the Referee allows the kick to proceed
- if the ball enters the goal, the kick is retaken
- if the ball does not enter the goal, the kick is not retaken
- if the ball rebounds from the goalkeeper, the crossbar or the goal post and is touched by this player, the Referee stops play and restarts the match with an indirect free kick to the defending team

A team-mate of the goalkeeper enters the penalty area or moves in front of or within 9.15 m (10 yds) of the penalty mark:
- the Referee allows the kick to proceed
- if the ball enters the goal, a goal is awarded
- if the ball does not enter the goal, the kick is retaken

A player of both the defending team and the attacking team infringe the Laws of the Game:
- the kick is retaken

IF, AFTER THE PENALTY KICK HAS BEEN TAKEN:
The kicker touches the ball a second time (except with his hands) before it has touched another player:
- an indirect free kick is awarded to the opposing team, the kick to be taken from the place where the infringement occurred*

The kicker deliberately handles the ball before it has touched another player:
- a direct free kick is 'awarded to the opposing team, the kick to be taken from the place where the infringement occurred*

The ball is touched by an outside agent as it moves forward:
- the kick is retaken

The ball rebounds into the field of play from the goalkeeper, the crossbar or the goalposts, and is then touched by an outside agent:
- the Referee stops play
- play is restarted with a dropped ball at the place where it touched the outside agent*

LAW 15 – THE THROW-IN

A throw-in is a method of restarting play.

A goal cannot be scored directly from a throw-in.

A throw-in is awarded:
- when the whole of the ball passes over the touch line, either on the ground or in the air
- from the point where it crossed the touch line
- to the opponents of the player who last touched the ball

PROCEDURE
At the moment of delivering the ball, the thrower:
- faces the field of play
- has part of each foot either on the touch line or on the ground outside the touch line

- uses both hands
- delivers the ball from behind and over his head

The thrower may not touch the ball again until it has touched another player.

The ball is in play immediately it enters the field of play.

INFRINGEMENTS/SANCTIONS

THROW-IN TAKEN BY A PLAYER OTHER THAN THE GOALKEEPER

If, after the ball is in play, the thrower touches the ball a second time (except with his hands) before it has touched another player:
- an indirect free kick is awarded to the opposing team, the kick to be taken from the place where the infringement occurred*

If, after the ball is in play, the thrower deliberately handles the ball before it has touched another player:
- a direct free kick is awarded to the opposing team, the kick to be taken from the place where the infringement occurred*
- a penalty kick is awarded if the infringement occurred inside the thrower's penalty area

THROW-IN TAKEN BY THE GOALKEEPER

If, after the ball is in play, the goalkeeper touches the ball a second time (except with his hands), before it has touched another player
- an indirect free kick is awarded to the opposing team, the kick to be taken from the place where the infringement occurred*

If, after the ball is in play, the goalkeeper deliberately handles the ball before it has touched another player:
- a direct free kick is awarded to the opposing team if the infringement occurred outside the goalkeeper's penalty area, the kick to be taken from the place where the infringement occurred*
- an indirect free kick is awarded to the opposing team if the infringement occurred inside the goalkeeper's penalty area, the kick to be taken from the place where the infringement occurred*

If an opponent unfairly distracts or impedes the thrower:
- *he is cautioned for unsporting behaviour and shown the yellow card*

For any other infringement of this Law:
- the throw-in is taken by a player of the opposing team

LAW 16 – THE GOAL KICK

A goal kick is a method of restarting play.

A goal may be scored directly from a goal kick, but only against the opposing team.

A goal kick is awarded when:
- the whole of the ball having last touched a player of the attacking team, passes over the goal line, either on the ground or in the air, and a goal is not scored in accordance with Law 10

PROCEDURE

- the ball is kicked from any point within the goal area by a player of the defending team
- opponents remain outside the penalty area until the ball is in play
- the kicker does not play the ball a second time until it has touched another player
- the ball is in play when it is kicked directly beyond the penalty area

INFRINGEMENTS/SANCTIONS

If the ball is not kicked directly into play beyond the penalty area:
- the kick is retaken

GOAL KICK TAKEN BY A PLAYER OTHER THAN THE GOALKEEPER
If, after the ball is in play, the kicker touches the ball a second time (except with his hands) before it has touched another player:
- an indirect free kick is awarded to the opposing team, the kick to be taken from the place where the infringement occurred*

If, after the ball is in play, the kicker deliberately handles the ball before it has touched another player:
- a direct free kick is awarded to the opposing team, the kick to be taken from the place where the infringement occurred*
- a penalty kick is awarded if the infringement occurred inside the kicker's penalty area

GOAL KICK TAKEN BY THE GOALKEEPER
If, after the ball is in play, the goalkeeper touches the ball a second time (except with his hands) before it has touched another player:
- an indirect free kick is awarded to the opposing team, the kick to be taken from the place where the infringement occurred*

If, after the ball is in play, the goalkeeper deliberately handles the ball before it has touched another player:
- a direct free kick is awarded to the opposing team if the infringement occurred outside the goalkeeper's penalty area, the kick to be taken from the place where the infringement occurred*
- an indirect free kick is awarded to the opposing team if the infringement occurred inside the goalkeeper's penalty area, the kick to be taken from the place where the infringement occurred*

For any other infringement of this Law:
- the kick is retaken

LAW 17 – THE CORNER KICK

A corner kick is a method of restarting play.

A goal may be scored directly from a corner kick, but only against the opposing team.

A corner kick is awarded when:
- the whole of the ball, having last touched a player of the defending team, passes over the goal line, either on the ground or in the air, and a goal is not scored in accordance with Law 10

PROCEDURE
- the ball is placed inside the corner arc at the nearest corner flagpost
- the corner flagpost is not moved
- opponents remain at least 9.15 m (10 yds) from the ball until it is in play
- the ball is kicked by a player of the attacking team
- the ball is in play when it is kicked and moves
- the kicker does not play the ball a second time until it has touched another player

INFRINGEMENTS/SANCTIONS
Corner kick taken by player other than the goalkeeper

If, after the ball is in play, the kicker touches the ball a second time (except with his hands) before it has touched another player:
- an indirect free kick is awarded to the opposing team, the kick to be taken from the place where the infringement occurred*

If, after the ball is in play, the kicker deliberately handles the ball before it has touched another player:
- a direct free kick is awarded to the opposing team, the kick to be taken from the place where the infringement occurred*
- a penalty kick is awarded if the infringement occurred inside the kicker's penalty area

CORNER KICK TAKEN BY THE GOALKEEPER
If, after the ball is in play, the goalkeeper touches the ball a second time (except with his hands) before it has touched another player:
- an indirect free kick is awarded to the opposing team, the kick to be taken from the place where the infringement occurred*

If, after the ball is in play, the goalkeeper deliberately handles the ball before it has touched another player:
- a direct free kick is awarded to the opposing team if the infringement occurred outside the goalkeeper's penalty area, the kick to be taken from the place where the infringement occurred*
- an indirect free kick is awarded to the opposing team if the infringement occurred inside the goalkeeper's penalty area, the kick to be taken from the place where the infringement occurred*

For any other infringement:
- the kick is retaken

Part 8

THE FINAL WHISTLE

Extra information to know the Game better

MATCH DECIDERS OR TIE-BREAKERS

THE TECHNICAL AREA – FOR COACHES

THE FOURTH OFFICIAL – WHAT HE DOES

MATCH DECIDERS OR TIE-BREAKERS
FOR KNOCK-OUT COMPETITIONS
Match Deciders or Tie-breakers came into football in 1970 to replace the unsatisfactory method of deciding tied matches, in knock-out competitions, by the toss of a coin. The system adopted by the International F.A. Board was a series of kicks from the penalty mark. The official procedure is set out below.

KICKS FROM THE PENALTY MARK
Taking kicks from the penalty mark is a method of determining the winning team where competition rules require there to be a winning team after a match has been drawn

PROCEDURE
- The Referee chooses the goal at which the kicks will be taken
- The Referee tosses a coin and the team whose captain wins the toss takes the first kick
- The Referee keeps a record of the kicks being taken
- Subject to the conditions explained below, both teams take five kicks
- The kicks are taken alternately by the teams
- If, before both teams have taken five kicks, one has scored more goals than the other could score, even if it were to complete its five kicks, no more kicks are taken
- If after both teams have taken five kicks, both have scored the same number of goals, or have not scored any goals, kicks continue to be taken in the same order until one team has scored a goal more than the other from the same number of kicks
- A goalkeeper who is injured while kicks are being taken from the penalty mark and is unable to continue as goalkeeper may be replaced by a named substitute provided his team has not used the maximum number of substitutes permitted under the competition rules
- With the exception of the foregoing case, only players who are on the field of play at the end of the match, which includes extra time where appropriate, are allowed to take kicks from the penalty mark
- Each kick is taken by a different player and all eligible players must take a kick before any

player can take a second kick
- An eligible player may change places with the goalkeeper at any time when kicks from the penalty mark are being taken
- Only the eligible players and match officials are permitted to remain on the field of play when kicks from the penalty mark are being taken
- All players, except the player taking the kick and the two goalkeepers, must remain within the centre circle
- The goalkeeper who is the team-mate of the kicker must remain on the field of play, outside the penalty area in which the kicks are being taken, on the goal line where it meets the penalty area boundary line.
- Unless otherwise stated, the relevant Laws of the Game and International F.A. Board Decisions apply when kicks from the penalty mark are being taken.

THE TECHNICAL AREA

When the role of the coach was formally recognized in 1993 it became necessary to define the location from where tactical instructions could be given. This was named as The Technical Area. Televised football usually shows this area as where the substitutes are seated.

The official description of the area and its use are quoted below:

The technical area described in Law 3, International F.A. Board Decision no. 2, relates particularly to matches played in stadia with a designated seated area for technical staff and substitutes.

Technical areas may vary between stadia, for example in size or location, and the following notes are issued for general guidance.
- The technical area extends 1 m (1 yd) on either side of the designated seated area and extends forward up to a distance of 1 m (1 yd) from the touch line.
- It is recommended that markings are used to define this area.
- The number of persons permitted to occupy the technical area is defined by the competition rules.
- The occupants of the technical area are identified before the beginning of the match in accordance with the competition rules.
- Only one person at a time is authorized to convey tactical instructions and he must return to his position immediately after giving these instructions.
- The coach and other officials must remain within the confines of the technical area except in special circumstances, for example, a physiotherapist or doctor entering the field of play, with the Referee's permission, to assess an injured player.
- The coach and other occupants of the Technical Area must behave in a responsible manner.

THE FOURTH OFFICIAL

- A fourth match official was originally required as a standby Referee, available to take over the duties of either the appointed Referee or one of the Assistant Referees in case of injury or illness.

The Fourth Official is now required to undertake a range of duties to ease the tasks of the three match colleagues. The role has become important in high level football as can be seen in the following description of duties and responsibilities.

- The Fourth Official may be appointed under the competition rules and officiates if any of the three match officials is unable to continue.
- Prior to the start of the competition, the organizer states clearly whether, if the Referee is unable to continue, the Fourth Official takes over as the match Referee or whether the senior Assistant Referee takes over as Referee with the Fourth Official becoming an Assistant Referee.
- The Fourth Official assists with any administrative duties before, during and after the match, as required by the Referee.
- He is responsible for assisting with substitution procedures during the match.
- He supervises the replacement footballs, where required. If the match ball has to be replaced during a match, he provides another ball, on the instruction of the Referee, thus keeping the delay to a minimum.
- He has the authority to check the equipment of substitutes before they enter the field of play. If their equipment does not comply with the Laws of the Game, he informs the Referee.
- He has the authority to inform the Referee of irresponsible behaviour by any occupant of the Technical Area.
- After the match, the Fourth Official must submit a report to the appropriate authorities on any misconduct or other incident which has occurred out of the view of the Referee and the Assistant Referees. The Fourth Official must advise the Referee and his assistants of any report being made.